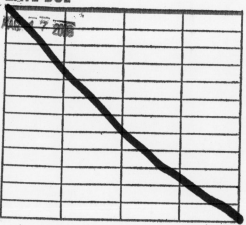

Oscar: An Inquiry into the Nature of Sanity

Oscar
AN INQUIRY INTO THE NATURE OF SANITY

PETER J. WILSON

Random House: New York

Library of Congress Cataloging in Publication Data

Wilson, Peter J
   Oscar: a man of the eighth variety.

   1. Old Providence Island, Colombia—Social life and customs.   2. Newball, Oscar Bryan.   3. Personality and culture. I. Title.
F2281.S15W55   301.29'861'8 [B]   73-3996
ISBN 0-394-48730-3

Grateful acknowledgment is made to George Braziller, Inc. for permission to reprint material from Saint Genet *by Jean-Paul Sartre, translated from the French by Bernard Frechtman. English translation copyright © 1963 by George Braziller, Inc.*

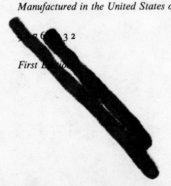

To Duncan and my parents

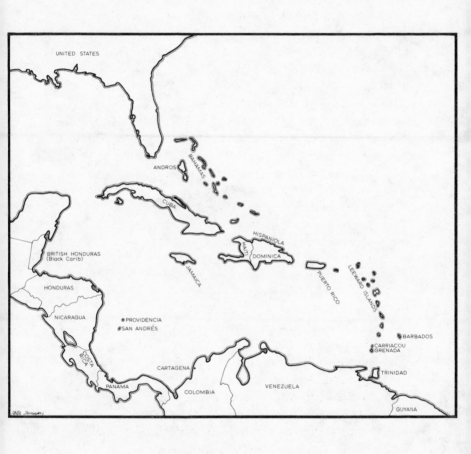

Hence, ye profane! I hate you all;
Both great vulgar and the small.
To virgin minds, which yet their native whiteness hold,
Not yet discoloured with the love of gold.
    That jaundice of the soul,
(Which makes it look so gilded and so foul).
To you, ye very few, these truths I tell;
The Muse inspires my song; hark and observe it well.
    We look on men and wonder at such odds
'Twixt things that were the same by birth;
We look on kings, as giants on earth,
    Those giants are but pigmies to the gods.
The humblest bush and proudest oak
Are but of equal power against the thunder-stroke;
Beauty, and strength, and wit, and wealth, and power,
Have their short flourishing hour;
    And love to see themselves, and smile,
And joy in their pre-eminence awhile;
    Even so in the same land
Poor weeds, rich corn, gay flowers, together stand;
Alas! death mows them all down with an imperial hand;
And all ye men, whom greatness does so please,
Ye feast, I fear, like Damocles;
If ye your eyes could upwards move,
(But ye, I fear, think nothing is above,)
Ye would perceive by what a little thread
    The sword still hangs above your head;
    No tide of wine would drown your cares;
No mirth or music over noise your fears:
The fear of death would you so watchful keep,
As not to admit the image of it, Sleep.
Sleep is a god too proud to wait in palaces,

And yet so humble too, as not to scorn
    The meanest country cottages:
    His poppy grows among the corn.
The halcyon Sleep will never build his nest
    In any stormy breast.
'Tis not enough that he does find
Clouds and darkness in their mind;
Darkness but half his work will do;
'Tis not enough: he must find quiet too.
The man, who in all wishes he does make,
    Does only Nature's counsel take,
That wise and happy man will never fear
    The evil aspects of the year;
Nor tremble, though two comets should appear;
He does not look in any almanacks to see
    Whether he fortunate shall be;
Let Mars and Saturn in the heavens conjoin,
And what they please against the world design,
    So Jupiter within him shine.
If of your pleasures and desires no end be found,
God to your cares and fears will set no bound.
    What will content you? Who can tell?
Ye fear so much to lose what ye have got
    As if ye liked it well;
Ye strive for more, as if ye liked it not.
    Go, level hills, and fill up seas,
Spare naught that may your wanton fancy please;
But, trust me, when you have done all this,
Much will be missing, and much will be amiss.

                    —Abraham Cowley, paraphrasing
                    Horace, *Odes,* Book III.i

Author's Preface

"No man is an Iland, *intire of itself; every man is a peece of the* Continent, *a part of the* maine."

These often quoted words by John Donne could well be taken as the text for the sermon that social science has preached to the modern world. But, as is the nature of sermons, it goes too far: it praises the dependency of men, only to forget their independency. At one time men were exhorted to labor for God; now they must work for Society. At one time clerics interpreted God's plan to man; now "sotheologists" reveal to us the function and purpose of social systems.

But as the unbeliever has outlived the rock-founded church, so shall the individual survive monolithic social structure.

I hope.

My study is of a single and singular individual. It is the story of his struggle for life as a person—a struggle pursued at every turn with those among whom he lives: his society. With birth comes a certain kind of life; but there is another life to be fought for after birth and before death. This is the fight I record. I might say, more in line perhaps with the language of social science, that this is a study of the relationship between an individual and his society.

The society is that of the island of Providencia, and the individual is Oscar Bryan. This is his real name, for I wish to reveal him, not hide him. In many ways, the study is a complement to my previous attempt to describe the relationship of a society to its members,* but while the two books are bound together, each is intended to stand on its own.

Oscar is an extraordinary person, and his life is not to be taken as one that is typical of lives lived in the Caribbean. Yet it is, to paraphrase Oscar himself, only through the study of the extraordinary that we can come to some sort of understanding of the ordinary. In the events of Oscar's life there is, I think, the exaggeration of what passes unnoticed, though not unsuffered, in the lives of ordinary people.

I tell this story as much as possible in Oscar's own words. These were sometimes tape-recorded, but by far the greater proportion of what he had to say was taken down in writing while he was speaking. When Oscar launched forth, he spoke in monologue and was often oblivious to those around him, including notetakers. At

* *Crab Antics: The Social Anthropology of English-Speaking Negro Societies of the Caribbean*, New Haven and London: Yale University Press, 1973.

other times I recorded skeletal notes, or I had to try to remember what I could and write up everything frantically as soon as I was able. The entire corpus of his utterances runs to several hundred typewritten pages, of which much material is repetitive and some quite incomprehensible.

From this text I have selected speeches, conversations, accounts of events, remarks and stories, and reassembled them. I have interpolated observations of my own, not only about Oscar but about other islanders whose behavior echoes that of Oscar, or serves as a foil for him. I have included some remarks and opinions passed by other islanders about Oscar and have re-created situations in which some facet of his personality was displayed. In some cases these are composite, being made up of aspects of separate occasions. Thus this is not a "true" account—it does not represent the sequence in which the information was gathered nor the actual order of events reported. Yet I hope that it gets to the heart, spirit and mind of the man and his condition more truthfully than a literal account would do. Do not misunderstand. Nothing that is reported here is in any way fictional; it all happened at some time or other, but not quite in the way I describe it here. This surely is no more a liberty than the "models" and "paradigms" invoked by my colleagues for whom the word "scientist" is more beguiling than the word "social."

I visited Providencia three times: from May to September 1958, May to September 1959, and December 1960 to March 1961—a little over a year in all. My wife Joan was with me on the last visit, and her presence altered my relationship with Oscar, while at the same time providing a different context in which my understanding of him could deepen and expand. He developed for her what I can best describe as a tender respect; had it not been for this, he would not have confided in us to the extent that he did, and I would not have been able to see him enter into a close (in his terms) relationship with a person other than myself.

I began taking notes from him and about him almost as soon as I arrived on the island. It was unavoidable, really, because he latched onto me from the beginning, and I was immediately fascinated. I soon became deeply involved, for in a frightening but illuminating sense, he became a part of me. I could see in him part of myself, as I suspect everyone on the island could see something of themselves in him.

It has taken many years to write this book, even though this may not be evident from its brevity. I wrote initially to satisfy—or perhaps I might almost say, to exorcise—myself. But as I became a little more detached from Oscar the man, and from the book itself, the possibility that it might have "meaning" for other people and for anthropology became more apparent and acceptable, and I let other people read it. They in turn offered encouragement, and I would like to thank them for this.

Especially I must thank Joan and my parents. Their encouragement rested on the intimacy and understanding of love, so that they knew as well what Oscar meant to me. It was Richard Elman who finally convinced me that it might have some merit as a piece of work, as a document that some people might be interested in reading for its own sake, if not for any other reason; and it was Ronald Schwarz whose enthusiasm persuaded me that it might be anthropologically worthwhile.

Thelma and Isaac Witkin knew what I was about, and it was their friendship that gave me the confidence —not just in this particular piece of work, but for other things too. When Thelma produced a portrait of Oscar from her reading of the book, I knew it was possible to convey something about him through the written word. Her picture is quite remarkable because it captures, as no photograph ever could, the mood and feeling of the man. Her portrait of Oscar, which is reproduced on the jacket, is an integral part of this book.

My visits to Providencia were financed by the Social Science Research Council, the Research Institute for the Study of Man, the Society for Research into Problems of Sex, and the Department of Anthropology, Yale University. I am of course solely responsible for all that is written here, but to these organizations and their personnel I extend my gratitude.

This book would never have been published had it not been for Helen Jackson—her encouragement and energy and a chance remark that made everything click. My thanks, too, to Mai Furlong not just for typing, but for helping in so many ways.

I have changed the names of everybody mentioned, except Oscar. The names are names common on the island, and if in spite of all my attempts to prevent it, some people recognize themselves, I hope I cause them no embarrassment or shame.

Peter J. Wilson
Waiora Farm
Dunedin
New Zealand

Contents

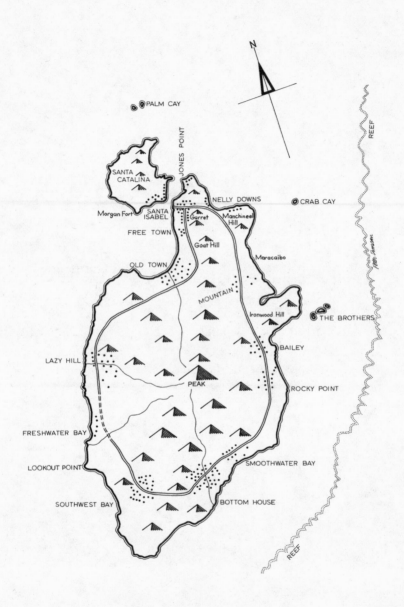

N

PALM CAY

JONES POINT

SANTA
CATALINA

NELLY DOWNS

CRAB CAY

Morgan Fort   SANTA
ISABEL   Garret

FREE TOWN

Manchineel
Hill

Goat Hill

OLD TOWN

Maracaibo

MOUNTAIN

Ironwood Hill

THE BROTHERS

LAZY HILL

BAILEY

PEAK

ROCKY POINT

FRESHWATER BAY

LOOKOUT POINT

SMOOTHWATER BAY

SOUTHWEST BAY

BOTTOM HOUSE

REEF

REEF

Providencia:
A Society

On the map the island of Providencia, or Old Providence, appears as a tiny dot in the southwest corner of the Caribbean Sea. But for those who live there, it is the center of the world, the only land in a universe of sea and sky. Its nearest neighbor is San Andrés Island, just forty-eight miles to the south, but there is little love lost between the people of the two islands. And as far as Providencia is concerned, Colombia, its motherland, might as well be in another world. Not only is it almost five hundred miles away across an empty sea, but throughout the one hundred and fifty years of their association, Colombia has almost totally ignored Providencia, leaving it more or less to fend for itself under the sometimes watchful eye of the *Intendente* in San Andrés.

To the people of Colombia, Providencia and its inhabitants are something of an anomaly, for they are Protestant, English-speaking, and a mixture of African

Negro and European white, whereas the people of Colombia are Catholic, Spanish-speaking and a mixture of white, Indian and a little African. The situation came about through a default of history.

Originally settled by English Puritans in 1629, the island's strategic position along the route of Spanish treasure galleons quickly converted the Puritans to pirates. Their preference for laying up treasure on earth at the expense of Spain soon had that country embroiled in a series of expeditions against the island, the third of which was successful. In 1670 Henry Morgan stormed the island, but managed to capture it only by trickery. From here he took off to sack Panama, carrying with him all the inhabitants. It was not until 1787, nearly one hundred and twenty years later, that Providencia was resettled, for the changing pattern of Spanish, English, Dutch and French exploitation of the Caribbean had reduced Providencia to total strategic insignificance.

In that year Captain Francis Archbold, a Scottish captain of a slaving ship domiciled in Jamaica, retired to Providencia with four of his Jamaican friends, their families and their slaves. Over the years they were joined by others, also from Jamaica, and by 1813 the population was over three hundred. Then in 1818 the island sprang to life: Luis Aury, a French soldier of fortune with his own private army and navy, made it his headquarters. He rebuilt the main fort and made St. Isabel a thriving community. From Providencia he pillaged around the Caribbean, taking advantage of the political chaos that prevailed at the time as the Great Liberator, Simón Bolívar, drove the Spanish out of their South American colonies. Three years later, Aury fell from his horse and died, and Providencia returned to obscurity. In 1822 the people signed a proclamation of adherence to the newborn republic of New Granada, later renamed Colombia; from that time on, although its precise political status has varied, the island has remained a part of Colombia.

But its distance from the mainland and its anomalous cultural make-up have served only to increase its insularity. What is more, the instability of political life on the mainland itself, which has persisted since Colombia gained its independence, has meant that governments have had little time for a small speck of land so far away.

Today Providencia and San Andrés form an *Intendencia,* with Providencia having the status of a *municipio.* The administration of Providencia is headed by an *alcalde* (mayor), who is assisted by various officials, all of them islanders. In the 1950's the central government in Bogotá voted funds for the development of the islands, but all of these went to San Andrés, which has now become a major tourist resort, replete with casinos, free port, water shortage and canned diet. Providencia in the meantime entertains but few tourists and has no hotel, but does boast a small airstrip and a rough road. There are some on the island who bemoan such backwardness and who long for the excitement that electricity brings. But there are probably even more who relish the virtues of the island's unspoiled beauty and tranquillity, and who are quite content to leave the problems of development—crime, sanitation, poverty and frustration—to San Andrés.

By any standards Providencia is a beautiful island. It measures only five miles by three at its broadest points, but its rugged range of hills gives it enormous bulk and variety. The highest of these, the 1,200 foot "Peak," stands at the center of the island. The hills are covered with thick secondary forest and smooth grassy pastures, where fat cattle and sleek horses graze. Between the hills the fertile valleys are checkered with gardens where people grow fruits and vegetables. The sensuality of Providencia is shameless. During the day greens and blues vibrate in the heat of the bright sun and in the soft breezes; then comes the evening transformation into seductive reds and erotic purples. At all times the air is quickened with the salty savor of the sea, with the live smell of animals, with the harsh, sweet, stinging scent of rotting fruit and drying copra. Then at night the languorous odor of frangipani takes over.

About two thousand people live scattered along the shore in one or other of the fourteen villages. Some are white-skinned, tanned to copper, with angular European faces; some are glistening black with the rounded features of the African; and most are a mixture. The historical pattern of their Jamaican English culture has been maintained to the present day, although more and more people are learning Spanish as the radio becomes a more ordinary item of furniture and as more islanders are compelled to seek jobs on the Colombian mainland, rather than in the Panama Canal Zone or the United States, as they did in the past. For virtually everyone at some point in their lives leaves the island to earn some cash, which they use to purchase lumber and furnishings for a house, and such manufactured articles as cloth, sewing machines, utensils, tools, cigarettes and beer.

6

The usual way for men to earn money is to get a job as a sailor, either on one of the thousands of small boats that ply between the ports of the Caribbean, or with one of the major Colombian or American shipping lines. There are many who settle permanently abroad, but most come back eventually to retire. The residents support themselves from their gardens and by fishing. They produce a surplus both of crops and cattle, and this is exported to San Andrés, which has a chronic food shortage.

Tranquil and sensuous though life is on the island, it is also frustrating, for there is little variety and even less opportunity to realize those ambitions that are engendered by the teachings of the church, the state and travel abroad. There are those with money and education who aspire to standards of respectability from which they claim superior status based on a supposed sophistication and equality with the bourgeois of the metropolis. And there are less successful, less wealthy people, who are forever hopeful on the one hand, resentful on the other. Over all there hangs a pall of ambivalence about who they are culturally. That which is their own is derided by the metropolis, while their affectation of metropolitan culture is considered gauche and primitive—by themselves and by outsiders. And shot through this pattern are the ambiguities and prejudices of race and religion.

Sociologically, life on Providencia is intensely personal. Everyone knows each other in many different ways. People must live with the burden of intimacy, and this results in a complex pattern of relations in which every right and duty is bound up with emotions in such a way that the whole presents a sense of ever-changing tensile dialectic—which I have called, using the island term, "crab antics." Like crabs in a barrel, people are forever seeking to climb out, but in so doing they pull each other down. Only the strongest can ever get over the top. At one level, the level bounded by the shores of the island, these are people whose struggle for self-realization is bound up in the pursuit of reputation, of honor, of a good name. At another level, which transcends the island to embrace the metropolitan culture, these are people caught up in the tussle for respectability, for position and class. The conflicting values of reputation and respectability impinge on each individual's hopes and ambitions, giving rise to a subtler, yet more pervasive version of crab antics.

Such then, in brief, is the society of which Oscar was born a member.

I first met Oscar on board the *M.V. Ray*, the ancient vessel that brought me to the island. He rowed out to greet the ship in a dinghy that he had borrowed—much to the owner's chagrin, I later learned—and on seeing me, both stranger and white man, immediately introduced himself as Professor Oscar Bryan de New-ball, and demanded to know who I was, and what brought me to these parts.

Excited and nervous—this being the start of my first anthropological adventure—and rather groggy from seasickness, I was somewhat taken aback by the imperious abruptness of Oscar's approach. After shaking hands and giving him my name, I stood tongue-tied. Fortunately, Oscar quickly moved away to speak to some of the other passengers and crew, asking them for the latest news, for details of the ship's cargo, whether the trip had been a good one, and whether the ship had behaved well. And all these questions were asked in the same loud, authoritarian tone of voice as if the questioner were nothing less than governor of the island. Shortly he disappeared into the wheelhouse, saying he must see the Captain about important matters.

A few minutes later I was taken off the boat and ferried to the shore. Half apologetically, my ferryman explained to me that I was not to mind, for it was only Oscar, who was mad. Then he quickly added, as if he had given a false impression, that I must also remember that Oscar was very intelligent.

Oscar was quite short, and his habitual stoop and rounded shoulders made him appear even shorter. There was a certain chunkiness about his build and firmness to his skin and muscles which gave notice of great strength and toughness. He stooped, but he did not sag. His head was large and crowned with tightly curled silver hair. His face was strikingly handsome: deep brown eyes twinkled in their sun-creased sockets; a soft round nose; a sensuous, toothless, full-lipped mouth that sometimes pouted, sometimes curled upward in a gentle smile. Then the sharp high cheekbones offset the roundness of the flesh, adding firmness and assertion. Finally, there was his voice—strong, clear and resonant, it established his authority.

During my first stay on the island, and again in my two subsequent sojourns, I came to know Oscar almost as well as one could know such a man. It was he who first went out of his way to show me around the island. He took me to the villages and into the houses, introducing me to their residents. It was he who first instructed me in the geography of the island, telling me the names of the hills, the valleys, the gullys, the tracts, the beaches, the promontories, the springs, the streams and the innumerable landmarks. He knew equally well the names of island plants and trees, fruits and shrubs, grasses and herbs, animals and insects, fishes and birds. He knew the names, nicknames and genealogies of almost every inhabitant. And he took great delight in teaching me all these details. After a while, and not without justification, he came to refer to himself as a partner in my researches. Often he would be waiting eagerly at daybreak outside my window, ready to begin the day's work.

Yet for all his knowledge, and for all the value of his instruction, there was a catch. I began to learn that not everything he told me was correct. And I might wait in vain for us to begin a planned project. It became all too evident that sometimes he and I were unable to meet on the same topic or set out for the same objectives with the same intentions and in the same direction. Only too often it seemed as if I was getting trapped into a dialogue of *non sequitur* or into situations of divergent intent. In retrospect, it seems as if we were two characters acting scenes written by Samuel Beckett or Harold Pinter. As I recall them now, I can be wistful, nostalgic and amused. But at the time it was nerve-racking.

Before dawn there would be a tap on my window. "Oh! Professor Wilson! Professor Wilson! Wake up! We must be around to Gulley and pursue our science!"

"Very well, Oscar. But *sshh!* It is still early and I have not yet eaten." This I would manage to say fairly evenly, having been startled out of my wits by his booming greeting.

"I too have not yet eaten, Professor. That is why I have come." Then at the top of his voice he would shout, "Ho! Ho! Ho there, Mistress! Have ye no manners not to feed the stranger at your door? You must feed the scientists of the realm."

His exhortation was addressed to Miss Ray, in whose house I was staying, and I am not sure who was more embarrassed—she or I. Anyway, having persuaded Oscar to wait, quietly if he could, I got dressed. I ate my breakfast, and Oscar insisted on his. But Miss Ray would not feed him in the house, so he ate on the verandah. Breakfast over, I said I was ready. But Oscar requested money for a smoke. After half an hour or so he returned with a packet of Pielroja cigarettes.

"Well, where are we going today, Oscar?" I asked.

No reply. Oscar had dropped off into a doze in less time than it takes to say a sentence. He awoke after a few minutes, only to begin preaching in pulpit tones. "The children of this house are a blight. There is no respect for the aged. Once there was a time if a youngster disobey or disrespect his parents, he dare not come back for fear of a thrashing. Now you can't tell who the parents are. There is much juvenile delinquency. There is much confusion in these lands. Even the greatest of nations are in confusion. All like these children here. Bastards. Who knows which is their mammy and which their pappy?"

"Oscar, if we are to get to Gulley and back again by evening, we must leave now."

"Professor, lend me a change so I can get you a papaya."

"We will get it on the way."

"Well, Professor, if the people of Gulley are in a

bad humor this morning, then the fish can give us cause for delight. I have promised to give a hand to Alejandro with his pots. A friend must be a friend—be like the stamp on an envelope that sticks till it gets there, or a frog that keeps on kicking till he churns the cream into butter."

In the end I went off to keep my appointment and Oscar went off to do I know not what. Perhaps he really did help Alejandro with his pots.

Oscar

"Professor Oscar Bryan Newball is born of pious people. He is the immediate grandson of Captain John J. Newball, the first circuit judge of the Archipelago of Colombia. From his early years he has shown signs to become an educator. My mother was a very industrious woman. She is born of the Hooker family—Ketran Good and Francis Hooker. Her mother was Philemia Hooker. She was also very ambitious. She operated in some capacity as a washerwoman and ironer, along which lines she made good and became famous as the best for her time in these arts of work. She had three children; three girls did my grandmother have. Two died at an early age. She was the public-law wife of Captain John J. Newball. My mother was the only one of her children to survive. The other girls passed away at the hands of the obeah women of Curaçao. They came to this island as dancers of the caribbinny dance, and they dance to other tunes, too.

Peter J. Wilson

They accuse my mother of laughing after them; being young and undeveloped she put the blame on her sisters Janie and Seraphine, as the ones who had laughed after the caribbinny dances. The three girls fell sick and my mother was the only one to survive.

"My father, a carpenter, farmer and sailor, seduced my mother against her will. Finding herself in the throes of another woman's man, she repented this until her last hour. My father was very innocent of books, but he was rich in the lore of nature and very proficient with his saw. He made his marks as a hustler and a very industrious man.

"But I determined at a very early age that I would improve beyond my father's capacity and be apt to associate my ideas with other men. I studied hard and was a poor sleeper. In my youth I followed the gardening or farming profession and became an eminent fisherman. I also studied shoemaking and raised cattle; and my pigs grew very presentable which envied the creed of the Advent people. They denounced my pig-raising, and I have decided to do away with industry, which I have lived up to strictly until today.

"I cannot understand why the people say I am mad. I feel free to do what I want to do. If I want to refrain I can refrain. I feel I am in possession of my mind. I become despondent thinking on things of the past. The best thing is to be busy night and day. I forget some of the stings."

At this Oscar lapsed into a long silence, which I did not feel free to interrupt with a question. He seemed to wrap himself up in the chair and the shadows. Suddenly he rose and shuffled through the room, out of the door and into the night, mumbling good night as he left.

The following day, Joan and I set off on horseback for Smoothwater Bay, about an hour's ride across the island from our house in Santa Isabel. The early morning was cool and moist around us as we clopped uphill and trotted down. At about the halfway point we stopped at Miss Bercita's store just past Mountain. We had a chat and heard all about Miss Bercita's health— her nerves were getting to her, she said, and her husband was, too. And the people these days were so vexing.

Bercita was a ponderous woman, thin-lipped, be-spectacled, and lined with the cares of a prosperous life. She had inherited a lot of land from her father, and she owned and managed her little concrete store. Her husband, Captain Barnaby, sailed the *Cygnet* between San Andrés and Cartagena, Colombia, carrying supplies for Cervantes's store there; every so often he resupplied his wife's store on Providencia. But Bercita was glad to see us and tell us her woes, and we spent an hour of our journey with her, drinking some lemonade and snacking on some coconut cakes before we went on our way to Smoothwater Bay.

We met few travelers, but we could see many people watching us from their windows. "Ya takin' a ride?" they would shout.

"Taking a ride," I'd reply.

"Where ya gwan?" they'd yell back.

"Smoothwater Bay," I'd answer.

They would nod and repeat, "Smoothwater Bay."

17

After we had passed, tiny, spattered, wide-eyed children would dash out onto the path to watch our progress out of sight.

We arrived at the Newton house at the height of the noonday sun, but in time for a lunch of sardines hauled fresh from the sea that morning and pressure-cooked in thick tomato sauce. Elder Sigmund and his family were delighted to see us, and they flustered and fluttered at our arrival, apologizing for their poverty and pleading their humbleness.

Elder Sigmund, so called for his position in the Adventist Church, was a tall but stooped man in his seventies who projected a gentleness that some, especially Oscar, implied was denied by his actions. His yellowed skin was crinkled with age and the sun, but his eyes twinkled behind his gold-rimmed spectacles, giving him the look of the intellectual. His thin lips were constantly set in a grin, but what capped the whole impression of mischievous, bumbling benevolence was the huge Mexican straw hat which he wore at all times outdoors, and sometimes, in his absent-mindedness, in the house as well. He was almost crippled by bursitis, but still worked in the garden, rode his donkey, worked in his little shop making brooms, and stubbornly (his wife's word) tried to do all the odd things that the man of the house is required to do. At times every other movement was accompanied by an involuntary gasp of pain or a whistled intake of breath.

Elder Sigmund's love, his passion, his obsession, was his religion. The most secular and innocent of conversations could set him off on an abstruse point of theology which would end up in a vindication of Adventist doctrine and an uncompromising condemnation of Roman Catholicism and its "perversions." A favorite topic of his was the prophecy, in Revelation, about the Mark of the Beast, wherein the Beast (the Catholics)— who is also Babylon, the mother of harlots, intrigue and decay—shall fall before the Lamb, those who have followed the ways of the Lord and who shall be saved, the Adventists. This, he argued, was further supported by the Book of Daniel, which also prophesied the fall of the Roman Catholics. He would happily spend an entire day arguing the point, especially if his audience was skeptical, like me. Evolution was another matter about which he could get wound up, and bogged down, in innumerable chapters and verses from the Bible, and in articles from the Adventist magazines.

Protestants were no more immune from his castigation than Catholics. He would rail against the perfidy of those Protestants who ignored the injunction to worship on a Saturday, and who gave themselves up to the evils of dancing, drinking, smoking, eating pork—to Sodom and Gomorrah. He led his family in Bible study and prayers first thing in the morning and last thing at night, but with such a gentleness and good humor that he was willingly followed. Sometimes his exaggerations would bring forth a "Pshaw! Come now, Siggy," from his pragmatic little wife, who believed as devoutly in her God as he did in his.

Smoothwater Bay is a small village of largish houses, and Sigmund's was the largest in town. The only house on the island to rise to three stories, it had proudly withstood the devastating hurricane of 1941, a testament to the skill of the builder, Elder Sigmund. It was now sagging a bit, the verandah floor was unsafe in parts, the yellow paint had almost peeled off, and some

19

of the shutters leaned against the wall. The task of repair was too difficult and expensive now, and anyway Sigmund's concerns had shifted to the problem of death and the difficulties it brings to life.

Sigmund's two sons, both of whom had recently returned to the island with their families, were living in rented houses down the road. Sigel, the eldest, had gone bankrupt trying to run a refrigerator agency in Bogotá, Colombia. He had, he said, been duped and cheated until he had no money left. He had come back to the island because it was the only place he could afford to live while thinking up new ways to make a living fitting to his station. The younger brother, Arthur, had come back from the seminary in Montevideo, where he had been a medical student. His funds had run out, and he had received no payments for many months. He said they had been intercepted by Sigel and used to shore up the latter's sagging business. So the brothers did not speak to each other and never visited their father's house together. Sigmund was sickened and mystified by their quarrel but could see no fault in either, and could never, I suppose, ever learn the truth of the matter.

Sigmund was trying to divide up his land among his two sons and his grandchildren, including the children of his daughter, who at that time was living in Venezuela. He would pore over the maps and the measurements of his lands, consulting first with Sigel, who would state his preferences and his plans. Sigel would say he wanted to have Cocomountain, and Sigmund would reply, "You shall have it, my son. And we must give Arthur Bush Pen." Sigel would reply that this was too good for Arthur, but let it go. Then Sigmund would confer with Arthur, telling him that he had decided to give Cocomountain to Sigel. Arthur would expostulate, "But haven't I always said I would love that land since I was a boy? That is where I would put my house to see the sun set on the glory of God every night." Sigmund would sigh and say he would then have to reconsider—which he did.

Sigmund's large house was honeycombed with tiny rooms, and we were given one of them. Joan stayed around the house with the wives while I explored the neighborhood with Arthur. The Newtons were having some difficulties with people stealing from their gardens, so one morning we went off to Spring Gully, where Arthur said "the baboons from Bottom House" had been "stealing our coconuts." Once there we set about inserting old razor blades in the trunks of the palms, placed a human skull (the origin of which I did not inquire about) on a branch overhanging the pathway leading into the grove, and sprinkled about a mixture that Arthur had concocted of various herbs, urine and chicken blood. We returned the next day, but more coconuts had been taken. Arthur despaired of the wickedness of the people.

Saturday morning Joan and I set out on horseback for the church in Rocky Point, accompanied by Elder Sigmund, Mistress Newton, their twin granddaughters, and Arthur and his wife. Sigmund was resplendent in a starched and pressed white shirt, shiny stiff khaki trousers, and a large Mexican hat.

The church was a small, white painted structure, very prim and neat, which sat on top of a hill overlooking the sea. We climbed the steps leading to the door, and there just outside sat Oscar, puffing vigorously at a cigarette (forbidden by Adventists) with a full packet jutting out from the bulging sack at his side. He took no notice of us as we entered the church, but every well-combed head turned as we took our places. Oscar entered after us, genuflecting and crossing himself as he took a seat in a corner, still smoking.

We had been invited to attend this particular service because it was the last to be conducted by Elder Jenkins, brother of John Jenkins, the island's leading merchant, businessman and politician. Elder Jenkins had spent a few weeks on the island but normally lived in the Panama Canal Zone. We were promised a good sermon. After some prayers, hymns and announcements, Elder Jenkins stood to give his sermon. He was prosperously dressed in a fashionable tropical suit, and his well-manicured person, pointed features and clear-plastic-framed glasses suggested a very proper fundamentalist Midwesterner. He preached to us the evils of dancing and drinking, drawing lurid pictures of the sinning rampant in the larger world outside. But the outside world did not have a monopoly on sin, he thundered: wickedness had come to the islands too. Were there not dancing and drinking, smoking and gambling right here on Providencia? Were there not those who right under our very noses were plunging into iniquity, following the devildries of Satan with great laughter? He condemned the Catholics and their lotteries and their condoning of promiscuity and their worship of idols. He condemned the Baptists for continuing to worship on Sundays when the Bible made it clear that Saturday was the Lord's appointed day. His sermon was punctuated by signs of agreement from the congregation and by loud amens from Oscar. For the final hymn Oscar joined in, but he sang off key and several measures behind the rest of the congregation. For the last verse his bass was absent; he had left silently.

After a few more days at Smoothwater Bay, spent discussing the meaning of the Bible, the problem of the land, and plans for the future, we returned to Town, leaving behind an invitation for the Newtons to come and visit us.

I won't deny the feeling of relief I had at leaving. There was an edginess in the Newton home. People were out of proportion to each other: objects, property and ideas seemed to get in the way of understanding. The institution and doctrines of the church plowed over Elder Sigmund's relations with his family; he could not understand that love does not follow just because one observes moral precepts.

The idea of learning, and being learned, stood in the way of both Arthur's and his father's comprehension of reality. In appearance and manner Elder Sigmund was the confident yet humble, correct but gentle intellectual convinced of his righteousness and infallibility. To him righteousness alone was rightness. Arthur, clever and learned, was so ambitious to be more so that he fell easy prey to the practice of cunning, guile and deception.

Upon our return to Santa Isabel we learned that Oscar too had made his way back from Rocky Point, and no sooner had I dismounted at Mr. Ray's store to buy a cold beer than Oscar appeared, coming from the opposite direction.

As usual, his back was bent double by the weight of his bulging sack, reducing his habitual shuffle to a barely perceptible plod. Slowly he turned the corner to the last stretch of road.

The white concrete of the road glared violently in the strong sunlight. Coming to the wall that formed the corner between Wing's store and the government office, he sloughed off his sack and sat down. Then he slowly and methodically drew out a papaya, breadfruit, coconuts, plantain and oranges, arranging them neatly along the wall.

"Yes," he said, "they are for sale."

Taking a cigarette from his shirt pocket he placed it between his dry lips, lit it with great deliberation, and as the smoke curled up around his face, wrinkled up his eyes. He stayed sitting there, hunched over his knees, until the gray cigarette ash, getting longer and longer, finally dropped off. He sold some of the fruit, always a welcome commodity in Town: a papaya to the Judge, some breadfruit to the Treasurer, plantain to Hamjy, who had popped out of his rum shop. After this brisk trade, and having shooed off some little children who stood staring, he lit another cigarette and then announced at the top of his voice, "I want nothing to do with the Campbell dirt." The Judge, the Treasurer, Hamjy and others who had come by stopped still. The sound of his proclamation brought bodies from doorways and heads from windows. "The Campbells in the village of Rocky Point are blighting the name of morality on this island."

The bystanders smiled, tittered a little nervously and looked furtively at one another.

"What nonsense is this you say, Oscar?" asked the Treasurer.

"Oh, Oscar! Him is mad this morning," observed Hamjy in his squeaky voice.

Oscar sat in silence, squinting at them quizzically. He was playing with them, waiting for their curious questions, knowing they would bite. Everyone looked casual and disinterested, but no one moved away. Finally the Judge inquired, "What nonsense is this? Which Campbells you mean?"

Everyone leaned forward a little to catch Oscar's reply. It boomed out. "Well, this morning I visited the home of one Joton Campbell, where I usually have some coffee when I am in these parts. We talk and exchange news."

"Oh! Him da ta'k a pile a' foolishness," squeaked Hamjy. "What you say happen, man?" Everyone made a half a step as if to go away, shifted to a more comfortable position, cocked an ear and waited.

"This morning," preached Oscar, "I visited Joton to take coffee, and was refused. Not only was I refused, but Joton came out with a machete and curses, threatening to kill me if my shadow darken his yard again. He keeps his daughter within doors these past months. She has not seen the sunlight since her belly grew big with the bastard she is bearing for Joton. Things is come to pass in this island that the people are already entered into damnation. I want nothing to do with the Campbell dirt." A long, hot silence. He spat out the butt of his cigarette that was stuck to his lower lip.

"Ah! Don't you mind Oscar, him is mad, *tscha!*" remarked Gimmy. "Oscar, how long you say she been shut up?" he shouted. He laughed as if he were joking with Oscar. Some people drew closer to hear the story again, perhaps with some more detailed embellishments. But Oscar had said his piece. Having sold his fruit, he left his sack and made his way through the crowd straight to Wing's store, where he bought some more cigarettes and quenched his thirst with some cold lemonade.

The bystanders stood around for a while and then went off muttering among themselves that Oscar was mad. But it was true, was it not, that no one had seen Joton's daughter for these past months? Hamjy went back to the rum shop and told his wife, who went over to tell Silvano's wife; the Judge told his clerk, who would tell his wife; the Mayor went home early to lunch to tell his wife. Soon everyone in Town—or on the island, for that matter—knew that Joton's daughter was pregnant with his child.

Oscar had finished his lemonade and was telling ancient Mr. Wing that he wanted nothing to do with the Campbell dirt. Through the store window I could just see Mr. Wing nodding blankly as Oscar talked on. Mr. Wing was not likely to understand too much. Nearly ninety years old and rather deaf, he hardly understood English and was really only interested in his store, the Chinese newspapers that he somehow managed to procure regularly, his daily meal of rice, and his great-grandsons.

I turned to walk back to the house and had gone a few yards before being hailed. "Oh, Professor, things are come to evil in these parts. You are going to dinner? May I join you?"

I waited for Oscar to pick up his sack and shuffle up the road after me. In silence we walked back to the house. As we walked he stopped every now and then to pick up anything that caught his eye—a twig, a bottle, a piece of linen. All of these were stuffed into the crown of his straw hat, which he carried cradled in one arm. Oscar's hat and his sack were his home, his portable self. In them he kept his furniture, his treasures, his worldly goods.

We entered the house. Oscar laid his sack down on the porch and sat in his chair by the window, placing his hat tenderly at his feet. Laura, our friend from Free Town, had cooked dinner for us. She laughed out loud and exclaimed, "Oscar!" Oscar chided her gruffly for her lack of manners toward her elders and told her to mind his appetite and her business. We all sat down to a superb supper of fresh-caught fish fried in coconut oil, boiled yams subtly spiced with ginger, and red beans. Oscar took his plate back to his chair, placed it on his knees, and began to eat. His toothless jaws worked up and down like a beak, his chin nearly touching the end of his nose. His brown eyes popped as he swallowed.

"Well, Missus, I guess you are well learned in the arts of cooking," Oscar finally commented. Joan thanked him for the compliment, but reminded him that Laura had done the cooking. He emptied the sugar bowl into his coffee and drank noisily. Sometimes if he had no coffee, he would buy a few ounces of sugar and pour it into water.

We all sat, smoked and talked about nothing in particular, but rested content in the pleasure of a good meal. Suddenly, with seemingly no obvious cue in what we were talking about, Oscar began to talk about himself.

"I became a devoted lover at the early age of

eighteen. My admirers were many and my girls not a few. When I was nineteen, mother brought me to justice for the amiable affair of pregnating one of her Uncle Sam's young chickens. She became my wife for eight years, but we strayed apart. She had poor aspiration. I married because she had trapped me. On my wedding day I was quite distressed in hearing another bewailing her loss. She has lost the boy of her choice and the inborn modesty of her youth at so cheap a price. For which we have both lived in a lamentable way and never forget what careless love may do. My wife was pregnated before the wedding day. I detested the delicacies that her mother prescribe. My wife had notions to become a coquette and I have morals that a coquette can defeat. I was too tender to foresee the end of the trail. No, I did not love my wife much, but to this union are born five children. I was not able to exchange ideas with her or to reason with her, and we strayed apart. While I was confined in the asylum at Corazel, my wife went into open prostitution, taking one Andrés O'Neill into my house and home and defiling my marriage bed.

"Mother, not standing for such immorality and abominations, drove them out as the Angel of the Almighty God had driven our first parents from their Eden home. To this union with Andrés O'Neill, a carpenter and Adventist, are born Garibaldi O'Neill, one branded with prostitution and christened with whoredom. His wife went from one degree of apostasy to another, until she had five or six bastards to her credit. The sympathetic-hearted professor sending after thirty-five years for her, she still refuses to come. He is now deciding a whirlwind of courtship and marriage as

28

King Ahasius of old, sending for his queen. She also refuse to come and is dethrone. And Queen Vashti— Queen Esther, rather, took her place, a woman to be her husband's voice. And a model wife and mother.

"I am old but I still have ambitions and aspirations. Still I will attain my end. Sometimes I think that I have found the woman, then I get cold feet. I guess it's the fear that the second will end as the first. Women usually respond to my eyes, but after a while they think I am from another planet."

Oscar's mouth opened wide until his eyes were quite closed, and he gave out a cackling laugh. "Then to those who open their door to me I say, 'Sorry, I guess I got the wrong door.'" He laughed again, shrilly. "Maybe my notion ideal of woman is too high."

"Yet there was one. She was married to another man and became his obedient servant. This I regard as sorrow to bear to my dying day. She has emigrated from her native homeland to bewail her loss and reflect her mistake of allowing a young man to touch the end of her fingers before he has a right to do so. God bless this dear girl, may Heaven superintend and may manna be given her in abundance till her dying day. For with her my love will always dwell even in the mist that separates us long ago. God bless all disappointed hearts, may comfort be given to bear their loss and shun the past of one who cannot bear his loss. So like Judas of old, he hangs himself up without hope of ever sharing in the human loss.

"There. A whole pile from my love affairs."

He gave an exhausted laugh and sank back into the chair. It had become very late. The kerosene lamps had been lit long ago, and their pale-orange flames threw dancing shadows on the wall to play some unrehearsed drama. Oscar's laugh seemed to die in his throat as sleep overtook him. This was how he went to sleep—never a preliminary yawn, but simply a sudden drop of the head. After a while the saliva dribbled past the long-burnt-out cigarette. He had probably not slept for several days and nights, for this was his way. He would remain awake until he could no longer hold his eyelids up. Once he had dropped off to sleep while eating a meal—the fork slipped farther and farther from his sleeping mouth, and the plate on his knees crashed to the floor.

"Oscar, wake up!" He did not stir, so I shook him vigorously. "Have a cup of tea before we say good night."

Joan brought in a pot of hot green mint tea and poured it into the waiting cups. I handed one to Oscar, who took it rather shakily. I offered to pour in the sugar, and he drank the tea noisily and quickly.

"Well, Professor, you are tired and I shall not keep you from your rest. Good night."

He rose rather unsteadily, stooped to pick up his hat, and hardly lifting his bare feet, shuffled slowly out of the house onto the verandah. There he arranged his belongings—taking all of his things out of the hat and the sack, and placing them carefully around him on the floor—rolled up his sack into a pillow and lay down to sleep.

When we opened the shutters the following morning, he was gone. On the doorstep lay a large, deliciously ripe papaya, payment for our hospitality.

As was the usual pattern after he bared himself to us, Oscar did not reappear for many days. While he was gone, tragic news came to the island—the *Magdalena*, the newest and largest vessel to call at Providencia and the island's hope for progress, had blown up at sea. She had recently left Providencia with orders from merchants and a contract from the government to ship kerosene and gasoline for bulldozers and government trucks. The telegraph message gave few details, and the shock of the event was made even greater by the speculation generated by lack of real information. Almost everyone on the island seemed to be standing outside the telegraph office or down in the square below the office, waiting for the next message. Many of the crew were from the island, and some people were expecting relatives to return on the boat. The next message that came through was that most of the people were dead, but no names were given. Another message an hour or so later related that the survivors had been picked up and were being taken back to Cartagena— but still no names. Griselda, Jason's wife, was rushing back and forth between the office and Miss Ray, jabbering nonstop about Jason being dead, and what was she going to do "now him gone?" Suddenly a small, dark-haired woman broke out of the crowd and ran shrieking up the street, screaming Spanish words that no one could understand. She was Eduardo's wife, a mainland Colombian and very much alone on the island. She was expecting her husband on the boat. The strain of suspense on everyone was immense, only partially relieved the next day when more details came over the telegraph. One person from the island was dead—Eduardo, who had been eaten by sharks. Another casualty had been a Colombian crewman. Two other islanders had been burned—Walter badly and

Peter J. Wilson

Jason only slightly—and Walter was in a hospital. All survivors would soon be on their way. There would be an inquiry.

I don't suppose the truth of what really happened could ever be known. One eyewitness said the ship just blew up, another said that one of the crew accidentally dropped a cigarette into one of the barrels of gasoline that the ship was carrying. Another version was that Jason was drunk and had taken no precautions about securing his cargo. The horror of the scene—fire on the water and the sharks grasping at flailing, burning flesh—was graphically described by those who had seen it and, in even more gruesome terms, by those who had been on the island at the time. For a few days there were tears and shocked faces, and no one talked about anything else. But as the tragedy receded, what had been a terrible accident was transformed into an act of sabotage, a plot for island detectives to investigate. In Hamjy's rum shop Doc, Carlos, Ronald and Alfredo discussed and probed: they must have got a lot of insurance for a ship like that, they suggested. " 'Em was out to get Jason after him run them in. Me think it was them damn Pais.* Them no like we from the island to run they ships, an' you can never trust a Spaniard man." Hamjy poured the drinks, and the men went on to speculate that Jenkins would still have a monopoly on the boats that came to the island, so perhaps he had something to do with the *Magdalena* blowing up. They argued and speculated well into the night.

I had thought that news of the tragedy would have brought Oscar around to Town. But whatever it was he

* Caribbean slang word for Colombians (also called *Panyas*).

was doing must have been more important, for he did not appear for some time. When he finally showed up he made no reference to the event.

He announced his presence through the window. "Good morning, Professor! Ah, good morning, Missus!"

He took a late breakfast with us, remaining outside on the verandah to eat. The belongings he had accumulated during his absence were arrayed on the floor, and he invited us to inspect them: several oranges, two small papayas, some coconuts, packets of coffee, small pieces of soap, three large nails, a paperback novel, stubs of pencils, several crusts of stale bread, a large rock, some sodden cigarettes, a box of matches, various assorted empty bottles, some pieces of fish that were beginning to reek, numerous leaves and plants, some pieces of colored cloth, and a lollipop. He had also acquired a change of clothing while away, and was now wearing a flimsy transparent yellow shirt over a more substantial one of bright red and two pairs of khaki-colored trousers tied underneath the knee with a piece of string. He was barefoot.

After breakfast he asked for an old razor blade and proceeded to shave the gray stubble from his face. Framed in the open window, he gingerly worked the bare blade around his chin and reported the latest news. "Well, sir, we have some scandals on Smoothwater Bay. If the Almighty God does not work on the Captain Attila's mind he is sitting today on a separation case. This Isabel his wife is become a common whore with Woodruff, Attila's brother."

He twisted his face from left to right as he began to shave his other cheek. "They are to give her a separation paper that Woodruff may take her away. But the captain is providing a cook and a nurse for Isabel and the child to keep her on the island. The stink is on this side, it is Barranquilla. Three nights in a hotel were Woodruff and Isabel playing their pranks, and now when it is getting hotter, they want to keep it a secret. Presumption is hell, after that comes paradise. Now Attila and I are brothers in afflictions."

He carefully wrapped the blade in a piece of paper and placed it on the floor. Clean-shaven, he walked into the room and sat down on his chair.

"These Johnsons are a kind of notable people, even in their adversaries and their adversities; they have been making their mark and are not foolish. You know the father is a very progressive man. That is exactly what the adversaries don't like about him. This is the only man that had a dollar, a live dollar, to put in a nigger's hand when he hires you. You don't need to go home for it, for he has it right there in the farm. But that is what the people doesn't like and that is why there is these scandals. For it is covetousness. That is the reason for quarreling. And covetousness is the head on which every other sin falls.

"You see, the higher a monkey climb the more he expose himself. That is how the Johnsons are. And some of them are just that way exposing their ignorance, like they don't know any better. Their culture is too low. They are not sufficiently developed. And they are a proud-minded people. They have an ambition to be in a certain grade sometimes when they are trying to hang their hat where they can't reach. Then they get involved and some of them get too dishonest. They hang their hat where they cannot reach.

"You have to find a hand that loves not covetousness. We have more disputes for land in this country than any other one case or subject. Well, it is this way, that the lands are the Almighty God and his son Christ Jesus double. By creation and by redemption. But we could only become steward. Yet we have all resigned our position to become owners. We don't have our stewardship any more. You have some men used to infest them into quarrels. All like this Captain Fred Johnson. Only two acres separates his lands of Freshwater Bay and his lands of Smoothwater Bay. That two acres prevents him from holding land from sea to sea. And that's the privilege of the only man of these parts. Captain Fred Johnson owning land from sea to sea. José Gomez was working these two-acre lands, but he was powerless to sell it, for it was really a servant wage of one of José's daughters. But Captain Fred was too glad to buy. Nineteen-fourteen is known as the year of the José Gomez murder mystery. Gomez was found in the hills above Spring Gully, dead. He was hauling a weed, and when they found him the weed was still in his finger. A bullet pierced him. You could scarcely see where it enter in, but, oh! did it bulge at the back of his head and tear the whole thing out. Gomez had talked his secret that the only way they could get him is they shoot him in the head. The night when the Gomez coffin was being made, Harry Hooker shiver like a man possessed of the ague and the fever. He was ill-at-ease. The old fathers took note, and they had some little ways of bringing Harry Hooker to see the dead and then the dead would bleed. So you know who had done the deed when you bring the right man there and the dead bleed. And Harry Hooker implicate Captain Fred. For his covetousness he was sentence to thirteen years and four months in the Cartagena jail and there he died. He simply kill and took away like Jezebel and Naboth's garden.

"We had a teacher in these parts, the Reverend Sylvanus May, says my people has the crab antics. You have a barrel of crab and they start to climb. But the one that reached the top height—all the other are pulling him back. If he ever reached the top, he'll simply have to be big strong crab. The crab antics. The hearts of men are getting in a lamentable way. We are losing the true sense of God and the reality that he is present everywhere. When the moon is shining they say the sea doth sit beside the moonshine on a dark night. We have something sometime you think is duppies.* But when you find out it is an enemy, not you. Making know the power how to weaken your nerves, as the arch rebel weakens the nation. That's one of the sciences, bringing down to their level.

"Well, I wonder the professor could lend me a change? I am smoking, and I have to go for that weed for you. Then I have to get some nuts, some for one, some for this and some for that. And from last year I have been trying to find a man to gather my nuts.

"Yes, I am going now. I'll be around tomorrow probably. I wanted to get you a little syrup. Then I thought I would go through to Miss Ethel tomorrow night and continue to Bottom House to the house of my uncle Julius Bryan and hit a nap and a chat with him. He is alone. He is about eighty years old but is still an important old man. He builds his graters, and I was

* Ghosts; the spirits who have lived and died on the island.

trying to help him boost the grater industry sometime back."

Taking the pesos I offered him, helping himself to my pack of cigarettes lying on the table, and picking up the bits and pieces scattered over the porch, Oscar slowly shuffled down the path to the road. Every yard or so he would stoop suddenly to pick up bits of rubbish and stuff them into his hat.

Captain Fred Johnson, whom Oscar had mentioned, had become a sort of folk hero on the island, a model "big man": a man whose reputation had transcended island constraints, who had wriggled out of the crab antics. As Oscar pointed out Johnson had become the first man ever to own land stretching from one coast to the other, but in achieving this notable feat he became responsible for perpetrating the first murder in living memory ever to take place on the island. He was known for his generosity toward those who worked for him, and he is said to have lived in great splendor in the largest house on the island—a house which still stands today after surviving at least one devastating hurricane. As a benevolent landowner and as the most powerful political influence on the island, he was known as *"el cacique"* ("the boss"). He earned his fortune, it is said, smuggling Chinese through the Panama Canal in oil drums and dumping them on the deserted reefs north of Providencia. Here they were picked up and shipped into the United States. Chinese were not his only cargo, however, and one story goes that he carried more than a million dollars' worth of emeralds, hashish and ganja (marijuana) on his most notable voyage. According to the islanders, he was once caught red-handed "fixing" something in Ecuador, where he was tried, sentenced and jailed for life. Undaunted, he escaped from prison, walked over the Andes and through the dense jungle, and reached Cartagena, where the astonished captain of one of his boats took him aboard and back to Providencia. "King Fred" was remembered as the great lover of twenty-nine "wives" and the father of fifty-six children. As many again claimed him as lover or father, but with less authenticity. His last wife, Miss Ethel, lived in the big house, crippled and bedridden, but still able to summon a gleam to her eye at the mention of Captain Fred.

The big house itself was crumbling, a fading testament to past glory. Some of Captain Fred's sons had done very well, but they had done so elsewhere in Colombia and had not tried to follow in their father's footsteps.

Captain Fred had been an old-fashioned hero, or at least his legend made him out to be one. Nowadays it was John Jenkins who aspired to be the *cacique,* but no one would grant him the title. John was a tall man whose thin features seemed to have been etched in his sallow skin like lines on a copper plate. He lived in the flat above his store, which was immediately opposite Mr. John's store. His house was virtually his prison, for no one ever saw him leave. During the daylight hours he sat behind a huge rolltop desk littered with ledgers and papers, and his only movement seemed to be to remove and replace his steel-rimmed spectacles. Everyone came to him; he went to no one. People who wanted to see him would enter through the back door and stand by his desk, which was in the rear of the store, but hidden from the view of anyone in the front. If he ever left the house to go anywhere on the island, it was at night.

Otherwise he left the house only to leave the island, sailing on one or another of his four boats. And now that the *Magdalena* had sunk, he had regained his monopoly over the means of supplying the island, for the only other boat, the *Ray*, was owned and skippered by Captain Jonathan, and he was more interested in being with his sweetheart in San Andrés than coming to his wife on Providencia.

Jenkins's boats served him well, though the condition in which he kept them showed how little he cared for them. One, the *Wintan*, was his flagship, a 75-ton, sixty-year-old hulk that looked as if it would go to the bottom during the first rough sea it encountered. But its brown-stained gray planks hid a brand new Cummins diesel that propelled it, when necessary, at speeds of up to eighteen knots, enough to outdistance the ancient patrol boats along the Colombian coast. The *Wintan* had possibly smuggled more commodities through the Caribbean than any other latter-day pirate vessel. Islanders told the story of how during World War II, Jenkins's boats had brought in barrels and barrels of oil; these had been buried on the beach, only to be dug up periodically, carried on board, and supplied to German submarines waiting thirstily outside the reef. While they were refueling the German captain would come ashore and have a drink with Jenkins and the mayor—and would pay handsomely for the fuel. A few days later, or maybe even the next day, an American vessel would arrive and anchor outside the reef. The captain would come ashore, have a drink with the mayor, and ask if he had seen any German submarines around!

The tales about Jenkins are innumerable and are

told with mingled awe and fear: how he ferried German spies to the United States, but dumped them overboard and kept their suitcases of money; how he allowed a stranger to erect a wireless transmitter on land he owned on Peak, in return for a great sum of money; how he searched the land registers to find out who had no legal title to his land and then made out one in his own name, thus becoming the "legal" owner by taking advantage of the illiteracy of the poorer people of the island. When he left the island it was inevitably said he was going to Bogotá to "fiddle" something or other with the politicians there. He had his henchmen on the island who did his work for him, and—so it was said—he paid one person in every village to keep him abreast of all that went on in that area. So even though he never moved outside of his house, he owned more of the island than anybody else and knew everyone's latest move or latest remark; he just sat behind his huge desk, insulated from the islanders by their fear of him.

Quite by accident I came upon Oscar one night as I was returning from a party. It was the night of the full moon, a time for parties, and by moonlight the island seemed unreal, with the flatness of a print. Houses were blocked out and became bulky shadows; trees appeared solid, black and lacking dimension. The water seemed frozen except where the ripples were spotted in the moonlight. The incessant, high-pitched hum and rasp of countless insects only seemed to make the night more silent. The heaviest, most tangible sensation of the night was the scent of frangipani, sweet, thick and silky, spreading itself across the senses. As I walked along the beach, feeling almost disembodied, I suddenly became aware of a figure crouching low on the ground. Oscar was on his hands and knees, slowly scraping together the debris and rubbish from the sides of the path into the center, where he piled it into small cones. On top of each cone he placed two twigs in the form of a cross. I watched him doing this for perhaps an hour, after which he moved over to the gullies alongside the road and proceeded to clean these out, too, leaving the slime in the middle of the road and piling the rocks and more solid rubbish across the gully to make a dam. He was referring to this when he'd told me at one point that he "served his people as scientist and engineer." "The people," he had said, "have no idea of sanitation. They are dirty. I now operate as chief garbage man of these parts. This is how to treat germ and plague. For I have been experimenting to see how theory and practice coordinate."

I remained in the shadows for a while; after I felt I had watched long enough, I backtracked and took a detour so Oscar would not know he had been observed.

Next day there was a hullabaloo at the far end of Santa Isabel. Ovideo and Maria had awakened to find all their clothes and utensils gone! Yet the doors were still shut and the windows shuttered. At the same time Mr. Forbes and his household had awakened to find somebody else's cups and plates on their shelves. And when they looked outside, they saw somebody else's clothes hanging on their line. But their own clothes were no longer there! The problem was quickly solved when Reyaes, who lived alone, stormed out of doors carrying a pile of ladies' clothes and yelling, "What de goddamn is dis?" and Cissy, a spinster, began screaming her head off and wouldn't come out because, it turned out, Mr.

Forbes's trousers and shirts were lying at the end of her bed.

Ovideo, Mr. Forbes, Reyaes and Cissy all found, in the middle of a room in their houses, a crude wooden cross stuck in a small pile of pebbles—a sure sign that Oscar had passed through during the night and had been the cause of the mischief. Of course, Mr. Forbes, Reyaes and Cissy were mercilessly teased by their neighbors. There was much playing at wounded dignity, much cursing and threatening of Oscar, but also much laughter. Some of the laughter may have been a little forced, for it was hardly comforting to know that one's house and person were so vulnerable to nocturnal intrusion.

Oscar did not come back to Town, which left me free to work on island records. But, as had happened before when Oscar was away, the island was suddenly stirred to excitement by an untoward event. This time it was the largest robbery in the history of Providencia.

Poor old Bercita's store in Rocky Point had been broken into and her entire stock of newly imported shirts, shoes, socks and cloth had been stolen. Captain Barnaby, her husband, had unloaded them only two days ago, and his boat was still riding at anchor when the thieves broke in. Oscar had gone to Bercita's house to tell her that he had seen the thieves galloping off with their loot. So Oscar went with Bercita and Captain Barnaby to wake up the Mayor, who in turn sent for the sergeant in charge of the police. After they listened to Oscar's story and Bercita's report, they went to the store to see for themselves what had happened. Oscar stayed there, but everyone else decided nothing could be done before morning, so they all went back to bed. By the next day new shirts were turning up all over the island, and the Mayor received a report that a house in Bottom House was piled high with shoes and shirts. But by the time the policeman arrived in Bottom House, the house in question was bare to the walls. Hamjy's rum shop and Mr. John's beer counter were full of men debating and detecting. Carlos said he was sure it was no one from the island; it had to be one of the road crew from the mainland. Oswaldo asked him, if that was the case, why "all them shirts was round in Bottom House." Doc asked Hamjy where he had gotten his new shirt, and Hamjy squeaked, "Don't you come funny with me, man." They speculated on how much had been stolen, beginning with an estimate of fifty shirts by Alfredo, but this was soon bumped up to "at least a thousand" by Enrico. Miss Bercita had come around to stay with her cousin Miss Ray, for she was quite distraught, and the two of them sat in rocking chairs on the verandah talking about the wickedness of the place and how the "black baboons was become so vexing." After remonstrating with the Alcalde that he had grown so lax in his office it was no longer safe to go to bed on dry land, Captain Barnaby had gone back on board his boat.

Then as suddenly as all the excitement had flared up, the subject of the robbery was forgotten. Many of the boys from other parts of the island were still appearing in Town with new shirts or shoes, and when asked where they got them, they replied simply that they had bought them. But no one said anything more on the subject. The mystery of the robbery appeared to have solved itself. I later learned that it was Barnaby's son, a mate on the *Cygnet*, who had organized and carried out the robbery. It was said he did this to spite

Bercita, who was not his mother. Whether or not this was the truth of the matter, I never could find out. I suspect it was known only to Bercita, Barnaby and his son. Oscar must also have known the secret, and must have seen what had happened, since he had alerted Bercita but he never told. He had returned to the store with the Mayor and the police sergeant, where he stayed several hours, and then went on his way to Southwest Bay to burn some charcoal, which he afterwards sold.

Whenever he visited Southwest Bay Oscar stayed with Miss Sevelon, a short, pear-shaped woman who was always highly made up, took great pride in her straight-haired coiffure, and was respected throughout the island for her kindness. Oscar spoke of her often. "She's a great chum of mine. Yes, for kindness, you go her way and she would never want you depart without eating or drinking something. She is a minister's daughter, but she had made a mistake, she thinks, for she has a man and a house, but they are a yoke. They don't mind the same thing as she. She has ambition for decency and higher culture and learning; but she goes the happy-go-lucky way. So I guess that type don't value honor so well. She has a big drag of children but she's pulling true."

When I visited with Miss Sevelon she often spoke of Oscar. She told how they would sit around the fire long into the night listening to him tell stories, or how he would come and chop the husks off her coconuts and clean her yard or do any task she asked of him. Once, she said, he came through the house in the middle of the night, took a large bag of flour and lots of eggs, and mixed them all together; the next morning, he told her that he was making a pudding for the whole family—

and that needed a lot of pudding! And once he dressed her little dumb boy in girl's clothes and the two of them danced and fooled around so much that everyone laughed till the tears ran. Oscar poured a whole bottle of perfume over himself—just stood there, she said, and shook it all over! "Oh! Oscar is a laugh, and him is intelligent too, man! Him know his Bible. But some time he is vexing, and then I think him rude, and then him is vexed, like he have devil in him. Him is a gossip too, man!" Miss Sevelon went on. "You has to be careful when Oscar is around. Him have a way of smelling out other people's rottenness. Sometimes some of the things he says you doesn't know to believe or not. Oh, he speaks of you around these parts, and I sure he speak of me 'round there. And since we doesn't know, we act accordingly."

I never could get Miss Sevelon to tell what Oscar said about me. She just assured me it was all good. I was not so sure.

Miss Sevelon was unusual in many ways. She was the only person of whom Oscar spoke that he never once maligned, and she was also the only islander who seemed able at all times to relate to Oscar with any degree of consistency and harmony. It was surely no coincidence that he characterized her as a mirror image of himself: she, a woman of intellectual ability unmatched by her husband, and he, Oscar, a man of intellectual ability unmatched by his wife. The irony of such a situation was not lost on Oscar—or on Miss Sevelon, for that matter. Such irony is typical of the view Oscar has of the relations between the sexes in general, and his story, now and later, constantly refers to women who reject true love only to find themselves rejected in turn by the one they love; or to the equally great agony of the true love who sees his loved one rejected by her new love.

What also seems to uphold the relationship between Oscar and Miss Sevelon is that she is a woman who never tries to hide from Oscar, or to hide anything from him. As far as I know, she has never showed him that she might be afraid of him. She has always insisted on being herself, and as a result Oscar always seemed more at ease, more relaxed and more "normal" in her company than with anyone else. She and her children seemed to gain genuine enjoyment from his company—which is not surprising since he was always good-humored with her.

Early one morning we heard bangings and shufflings on the porch outside as Oscar put his house in order. We quietly closed our bedroom shutters and quickly got out of bed before Oscar demanded entrance and breakfast. No sooner had we finished dressing, rather hastily, than there came the first bang on the door accompanied by a loud "Ho!" I opened the sitting-room shutter and Oscar came over and framed himself in the open window.

In his hands he carried a bouquet of flowers, simple in their elegance and tropical in the intensity of their colors. He offered them to Joan with his eyes, and then shyly handed them to her. He laughed nervously when she thanked him and remarked how beautiful they were.

"That's a vervine. Good for children and for the blood.

"This is a marshmelon. That is good for bladder

troubles—heat in the bladder, that's a condition. Heat in the bladder. Here is parsley and good hog feed."

There was a long pause.

"*Bueno!* I guess I can spread out my things. So hit a black note. Ah! Ye have many fruits."

"Oscar, would you like some coffee?" I asked.

"Yes sir, I would be glad to take a cup of coffee.

"Well, these flowers are puss. These flowers are green rose, and yet they look much like if they were mad.

"These flowers are omens and green perch. Don't neglect them, take the red. This is a hibiscus, but we call it a pup. This is purple, the sign of mourning; this is the mint when we are becoming too full. This tiny little one will wait for a name.

"And this is the weed Rangoon Adushaland * that I cultivate around my possession. Well, sir, it's a very good weed for sore throats and for colds and suchlike ailments. It is a good weed for obeah. It's a good weed to have around. There is the physic nut and the Chiney root, for strengthening the blood. Here the dandelion for curing the malaria.

"Some of our lovers have a way to use animal and plant life too. I've heard it said that the fresh cane juice and lime makes the boys frisky.

"Some of our boys have a way to measure themselves against a piece of yucca. Then the yucca is planted and as it grows so does the boy's manhood. Fish and turtle make you hot. Take the organs of a turtle and soak them in rum. Scrape the organs into the rum and drink it. You must scrape down, not up, for if

* Caribbean term for marijuana (also called *ganja*).

you do you cannot lose the erection. This is only for men. Fish is for the men and women alike.

"Sometimes when a boy likes a girl and she looks the other way he tries for a hair of her head. Then he takes a gold-eye needle and threads her hair and one of his and sticks the needle in the root of a small banana tree or a plantain. The more the tree grow the more she loves him.

"Here is some more foolishness for the women to make the man love. Wash under the arm and mix the water with lemonade or tea or something to make the man drink. If there is the chance, it is good to sew private hair into the underwear of the man.

"One day you shall hear more of our counterfeit science. For if you don't have a genuine science you have a counterfeit science. This is known as necromancy in the old times—spiritualism in the modern times."

Oscar lapsed into silence, taking out a bent cigarette, lighting it, and wrinkling his eyes in the blue smoke.

He came in, sat in his chair, and drank the coffee we offered him, dipping his bread into it. He stared straight in front of him as though he were watching his thoughts "traveling on waves," as he once put it.

While we sat there in silence we heard a distant shout. Then from in front of the house the shout came again, this time loud and clear. "Grassy dead. Burying ten o'clock tomorrow." The rider galloped on, his shouts receding.

The tinkly bells of the small church began to toll the number of the years of her life. They were all too few. Oscar sat there listening, and when the bells finished, he said, "Thirty-two."

Grassy was Graciella, a white woman born and bred on the island, who had made several mistakes in her lovelife. She had first married a Spaniard from the mainland, who had left her after she had borne him a son. She was very young, but the law would not allow her to remarry, so she lived with another and had his child, too, before he left her. This time she was in love with a sailor, but he had been gone for many months and she was carrying his child, her third. She was anemic, and after her second baby was born, her doctor had warned her that she should have no more children or she would die. But she believed, like everyone else on the island, that "a woman should have as many children as are in her belly." Now the bells were telling us that the doctor had been right after all.

Everyone in town liked Graciella because she was kind and full of love. She worked in Samuel's store; because Samuel was a cripple, she had to work very hard doing everything while he sat and directed her. But you could always go into the store and have a pleasant chat with her. Her children were always well dressed and minded their manners and did well in school. They clung to her, and she wrapped them in a warm, motherly love. Now she was dead, although her little newborn baby was alive and crying. People from all over the island were gathering at her house; as they sat down, they began wailing over her corpse. The clock was stopped in the house and a black cloth was thrown over the mirror. Some of her older female relatives began to wash the body. Others sewed a new white dress for her. The men brought benches and chairs for everyone to sit on; soon large urns of coffee were available. Eddy and Leopoldo came to collect the wood that Graciella had set aside for her coffin. There in the corner of the yard they set about making the simple white box.

Oscar had long since risen, saying he would be needed at the house of the dead. He joined the throng that sat there throughout the day. He tidied up the yard, moving from group to group to join in their conversations and hymn-singing. The little horse pasture in Town was full of animals that had brought mourners from all over the island, and their whinnying became more frantic the longer they were neglected.

The mourners sat through the night drinking coffee, wailing, singing hymns, telling stories and paying their respects to the dead. Oscar flitted through the assembly, comforting here, entertaining there, now singing a hymn, now telling a story—his presence, for once, greatly appreciated.

As dawn broke the following morning, the day of the burial, Oscar and I left the house of the dead and went to the cemetery, where Florentino and his friends were digging the "hole." They fortified themselves with jokes, stories and rum. As the hole got deeper, Oscar sat on the edge of the grave and entertained them with stories. In a few hours they had finished digging. Florentino rested his chin on his spade and stayed at the bottom of the grave. Oscar moved atop the mound of dirt at the grave's edge and stared downhill, across the cemetery pocked by small gray stones and mounds, and out over the smooth blue sea. There they waited for the funeral procession.

It was the largest procession anyone could remember. It slowly snaked its way from Grassy's house in Town, along the dirt road at the base of Marshall Hill, past the wooden schoolhouse and the brown and yellow clinic, and then uphill a little to the cemetery. As the white-clad mourners came through the flimsy archway that marked the entrance to the cemetery, Florentino hopped out of the grave, and Oscar moved to a corner of the graveyard. The bearers laid the coffin down alongside the grave, and everyone else separated and stood around in a large circle. The small, bearded priest, perspiring in his thick robes in the hot morning sun, came forward to the edge of the grave. The sun seemed to grow hotter and brighter; the brown skins glistened and the white clothes dazzled the eye. The green of the cemetery seemed to join with the blue sea and sky. The priest peered short-sightedly through his thick-lensed spectacles at the small prayer book in his hand and began the service in Latin. His thin, lisping voice seemed to evaporate in the shimmering air. He was not of the island, and Latin was not the language of the islanders. How could he know what the death of an islander meant?

The bearers sweated and grunted as they slowly lowered the coffin into the grave. There was silence as the priest prepared to deliver the oration, but as he spoke only Spanish, very few would be able to understand what he said. He began timidly, then paused for breath. As he paused, a huge voice seemed to burst in the air and descend over the assembly.

"By their fruits shall we know them, that is my text and by this shall ye judge. By their fruits shall ye know them. Some for this reason and others for reasons more than one and yet another for reason simple. All like Graciella that we now lay to rest that has lost confidence in men and Christianity, but not in God. But the Almighty God must do something about this thing we must call Christianity and a form of vanity; they have departed from the true sense.

"They have departed and lost the true image of God in their souls. Nothing can appeal to them. The voice of the little children crying for bread? But no. I can't understand it at all, how men claim to be made in the image of the Maker and Creator can be this instrument. Something is going on radically wrong in our world.

"I don't know what to say, but the Scriptures say in Revelations. Revelation—I wonder ye know the book? I know thy work, that thou are neither hot nor cold. Would God that thou were hot or cold, but because thou art lukewarm I will spew thee out of my mouth. The Catholic translation says I will vomit thee out of my mouth. Lukewarm. The Almighty God is taken to the heart. Spew him out of his mouth. That's why he can become this brutal, hear now? That's the only reason how they may come this brutal. The spirit of the living God is imparted, that what's happening to our world, the spirit of the living God is fast being withdrawn.

"They live in a state of concealed iniquity and sin. 'They shall not prosper,' thus saith the Scriptures. He that covereth his sins shall not prosper, but whoso confesseth and forsaketh them shall have mercy.

"Well, the only thing can help you is you're a prophet. Jesus Christ weeping over Jerusalem that killest the Prophet and them that are sent. How oft would I have gathered thee, as a hen gathers her brood under her wing. But he would not. Behold the house is left unto desolation, and I was making a survey to see whether Jesus Christ has returned unto that desolate place. I can't find it. I can't find Him. No wonder He can do all this. See how? No wonder He can do all this, and more too. Led by the spirit of demons.

"Grassy lying there, led by the spirit of demons. She gave them much respect and she had a reverential tongue. Now she is fallen into rest, but she has given many councils to guide the mischievous footsteps and to shun the rut. She said, 'Son'—when breathing out her last—'see these men leaving their own wives, may you never enter into that.'

"The religion of our Lord and Savior Jesus Christ liberates men and does not harness them behind asylum walls, nor mash up their families. Nor like this sweating priest here, the pirate of Rome and government that speaks in behind-the-back language. He must learn better how to adapt himself, being a fool with the fools and a fisherman with the fishermen, and in every way to cooperate and operate.

"And maybe we'll divorce, we'll separate till they shall find the right woman of their choice to build a nation. God bless our sons with moral minds. This is their privilege, but with mothers modeled whom their children may call blessed, their husband and father present, for they are the best. By their fruits shall ye know them."

Oscar stayed around for a week or so. He never spoke of Graciella, the funeral or his oration. He spent his nights sleeping on our porch and his days perform-

vigoration. Some of our saddest mistakes is to eat food that is not vitamized. We have some things that are substitutes, but the people know nothing about it and you can't show them. But we'll keep picking away. Well, well, I guess I am going to turn my foot round and pick a piece of fish. I want something fresh. I am going over the hill, Goat Hill, Garrett and Mountain Bay. And I guess some day you may give me a chance that I may prepare some homemade dishes. I used to cook for Mother, but that was great fun. They were the farm years, and I the only son. Yes sir, some of the things I did were strictly for women, but as it's Mother, I did them. Mother and I labored together, then she got marry and the house fell to me. I had a home from eighteen years of age—the girls are too easy on me then, for I had a cage!

"When I was a boy I earned twenty cents a day and help Mother pay the carpenter bills for a cottage at twenty cents a day. Then came season time. My gauge was ten tins of five gallons of syrup. When I made that I quit."

So saying, Oscar went off to get his fish and in less than two hours was back to begin cooking us a meal. We had no intention of trying to stop him!

First he took the broom and swept the kitchen, leaving all the dust piled in the middle of the floor. And there it stayed. Then he washed up the pans (which were quite clean), the stove and the food. After which he poured dirty water over his head and rubbed it in vigorously.

Then he prepared the meal. Some of the fish he stewed with onions, ginger, salt, pepper, herbs and sweet potato. The remainder of the fish he cut up into small chunks and fried in coconut oil. The peas and beans he stewed in a separate pot with some mint. In no time at all, the house was filled with a marvelous aroma.

Perhaps partly in retribution for our former impatience, Joan and I decided to make this a festive meal, a true feast. We laid a clean oilcloth on the table, arranged some flowers in a bowl as a centerpiece, arranged the plates, cutlery and glasses according to the best etiquette, and to cap it all, broached a bottle of Phospherine Tonic Wine. Oscar carried in the pots with pomp and triumph and insisted on serving us. With plates piled high, and glasses full, we sat down to a meal of small pretension, but great fulfillment. Oscar, having crossed himself very deliberately, hauled out a large piece of rag from his pocket and tucked it ostentatiously beneath his chin. We ate in silence, appreciation and contentment. Oscar could not put the food into his mouth fast enough, and after several servings was finally full. His jaws kept making chewing motions for some time after he had finished his food, and the silence was broken occasionally by his belches of satisfaction.

We staggered up from the table and sat down in our accustomed places to drink coffee and talk. Oscar was consumed by the moment, and gave us some of his favorite recipes. "We have a cake called the Rocky Point cake. You soak the cassava and wring it dry, then pound to a flour; add some spices, some cinnamon, ginger and some nutmeg, milk and eggs. This was one of the delicacies of my uncle, Francis Newball, which my mother used to ship to St. Andrews for him.

"The cassava johnnycake is made when the starch has been extracted and the gut is dried and made into a flour. To this you add some milk from green coconut and some butter. These are also delicious and delightful to the taste.

"Another is cassava cake, which is yucca squeezed out to dry with a cloth, extracting some of the starch, dried and pounded to a flour. To this you may add an egg, butter, spices and cinnamon, cane syrup and then bake in an oven with fire under and above. It is now fit for the taste, but not so much exercise for the teeth. It is very soft.

"Bammy is also wrung from the cassava and grated and rubbed on a sieve. When it is wet, it is soggy; when it is dry, it is more crisp. To this you may saturate butter and eat with fry fish and gravy.

"Cassava makes porridge, the sweet cassava, grated and rubbed on the sieve and diluted in a pot of hot water to which you may add fresh milk and sugar to the taste. From this you extract the porridge or the pap. When it is not heavy, it is the pap. Take a plantain instead of the cassava and you get it the same way— called fufu.

"Then you have wabul—porridge made from ripe plantain to which you add the cream of coconut milk. It is now delicate to the taste whether you add sweet in this state. Coco dumplings, which is what the Pais call 'patacon,' is fry plantain, crushed and fry again, and add spice and salt to taste."

Oscar drank his coffee and smoked cigarettes and seemed to float in his chair on a cushion of well-being. While he was sitting back in complete relaxation, a smile broke the repose of his face and his soft brown eyes began to glow with a warmth of reminiscence.

"When a child I was born and lived in the village of Rocky Point. From my early youth I was much inclined to be a Christian. I was a diligent churchgoer then to the Baptist church. At the age of six I decided for Christ. My grandparents were pious people; they taught their children to respect the aged and mothers of minor years. We labored as a united family, some to their net, others to their machete. We cultivated and was fortunate to produce our own food, the fisherman to catch the fish.

"I grew up with the sons of Askalon Hooker and his daughter Leodicia. We lived practically in the same yard, but our house was apart. We played together when I could spare a little time, but they seemed to have time to play all day. In those early times, life was not a burden as it is today. Everything was plentiful and cheap. A bag of yam were change for a bag of yucca, a bunch of banana could be had for a bunch of plantain, and no one made a fortune at the net and fishing trade—fish was actually plentiful and free. Our biggest ambition was that every mouth be fed. Our mothers would wash while our fathers did plod. I used to do herding and farming.

"So I would happen to meet them if I visit; this I did, but early found out that I was better off if we did not meet each other in such capacity as a visit among brethren. They were contentious, but I tried to steer clear of this, so my visits were few and far between. But in my teens I worked with them plying the blue Caribbean and visiting the Bull's Mouth and Colón. We went to Nicaragua and had a change if we visit with the Coral Reefs of Colombia, Quitasueño, Serrana Bank,

Roncador Reefs, Silk Cay and also Logwood Bay—a system of coral reefs up the northern boundary of Catalina.

"My mother would take me to the plantation and I was supposed to hoe my own row. I guess I was just eight years. My father had a plantation, but he had other sons and daughters, apart from us, so his interest was in them and not in my mother. So I grew, as it were, isolated from my brethren. We grew with little sympathy for each other because we had never played together, nor in any way felt ourselves to be on the same level. I guess I was very happy as a child when I was supposed to be catching my snappers, grupper, hogfish and other fish. I would sing songs to the tune of the early mornings and the setting sun. I still sing sweet music though I am not permitted to relieve my appetite —I still feed on the bones."

We sat silently for many minutes, which felt like hours. Suddenly Oscar broke in on his own reflections.

"But my gardens were always no less than one acre. They ranged from the highlands, lowlands and the plain. My lands from inheritance ranges from sea to summit. My gardens were a model, producing much bread for the eater and seeds for the sower. I ate not the bread of idleness which some can afford. They are loafers, but our motto is 'Progress is man's only distinctive mark.' My yuccas were soft, my yams delicious, but my orange vitamize and strengthen. My pumpkins were large, for my seeds fell in good ground. My melons delighted your eye for they became beautiful red. Their colors are green on the outside. My calves were fat, my pigs grew fat. May God grant that I may always be consented to labor with my hands, determined to wear out rather than rust out. My sons and daughters caught a flicker of their daddy's industry—they are no beggars when given the chance; they work with their hands and their brows get wet.

"At an early age I decided to take a change to the mainland. I emigrated to the Isthmus of Panama to study and to work. Daddy said my education would not be any use to him. I pitied the old man, for education was very absent to him. However, this only let me plod the harder and study industriously to make myself not so dependent to brothers, father or sisters.

"As a boy I drove the bulls, the heifers and the she-cows. I enjoyed at an early age the trade to be a shepherd. I loved the cattle, but I did chastise them and break a foot or two that they may walk straight.

"In the evenings we came home together for repose, rest and recreation. The ring we play and some sports around this place here. We had some girls would hold hands and inside the circle some big strong fellows jumping to break through. They dance to the tune of the latest fad—the caribinny dance. Then there was the cutout—that's an awful dance—you will be trying to see which of us is making the best steps. That will take spinning out and coming back. We also had the schottische, which lasted to this day. In these old customs and dances the people used to come together. Some from Old Town, others from Bottom House. The Hookers of Rocky Point did the entertaining and the Brittons did help. They would come from Manchineel Hill and the vicinity around Bailey Chapel, the big chapel in Newball's Bay. Then those old people coming down would wait over and visit until actually twilight, when they did find they are aboard again. They used shank's mare, for their foot were fat and their joints so big they could trot.

"They kept their Christmas from November fifteenth to January fifteenth, when they decide to go back to work. Around Christmas they'll come down and spend a whole week or so—nothing but dances. If the dance was made in Rocky Point, then next week in another place. But wherever the dance was, they came together united, as in a sisterhood. The cane-grinding time was also a big time. They would begin in February, but end with the rains. The seasons were more regular and life was more entrancing than it is today. The old days were saner and safer. Today we long for the days of yore.

"White and color mix better then. Yes, the color of the white did mix. The white men take to themselves daughters of the slaves. They took them as wives. So that's how it is. The purity we have depart from, so they reproduce what is called the 'mulatto,' the mixture of the white and the black. To this end our sons live up strictly till now.

"We have no prejudice then, as the whites of other lands maintain. We were men among men. But there is some here today. Yes sir, we have some poor proud— they hardly know what they stand for. And this band of poor proud, as we call them, don't even know what they stand for. Sometimes they are on top, other times they are below. They change like the wind, so to know where they stand, you simple has to determine the point from which the wind is blowing. So you may know how and where they stand. Such culture is not the best for our good.

"Rocky Point was much different then. We build

our own houses from timbers we had made. The roof was all thatch, and grass cover the top, but snakes love the shelter and the warmth that our grass affords. The rats were so many our fathers saw fit to introduce the Coomler* and the cat.

"Then we had some fellow from the Jamaica Island who enhanced this port. We were happy in our isolation, knowing so little of the wide world. Some Jamaicans would come out to these parts as teachers, farmers, medicine men, or even obeah men. Some of them would stay on, while others stayed not so long. Among them were shoemakers, teachers, tailors, musicians, swindlers and obeah. They come to make a catch out—going to some place where you can pick up a little funds quickly.

"We had one of them—the Reverend Johnson— operating as a preacher and teacher. He was degraded with an impassionate love. He became infatuated with the woman he call Sister Mercy, advising Brother Henan that the ram don't suit Sister Mercy. Sister Mercy need a schoolteacher and minister, he would say. He finally came to his last as a broken, unfortunate lover. He has never succeeded to marry Sister Mercy. Sister Mercy is married to Mr. Alcana Hooker, who saw fit to desert her for not meeting his ideals concerning a wife.

"But then we get some money sharkers, and that change the custom. The people has become modernized. The Panama Canal is responsible for this. People went there to work and some of our boys didn't come back yet! So they live and they die till their pension come along. Such is the shifting and changing of time.

* A mongoose.

Peter J. Wilson

"We are mostly dependent on our crops. There was a time when the gungu peas was our greatest industry. In the olden years there was cotton. Their best sport was cotton-ginning time. So it was found by man and beast. And the gin was the delight, the tasteless beverage of the men of yesterday. Today it is different. We love the import things, but not like our own product, the jump steady.*

"In the other times, the anxiety of today is mostly spare. The times is come up to no matter how much money you make you are up to the same place—hand to mouth!"

Oscar had talked for hours without a break. The burnt-out cigarette was still stuck to his lower lip; it must have burned him some time ago, but he never noticed. It seemed that the furrows and creases of his face had been smoothed away as the past in all its clarity and confusion ran through his mind. His rough dark skin had become the rounded, burnished flesh of a young man, and his eyes—eyes that sometimes seemed to hold in them the accumulated disillusionment of mankind—had become the dancing, inquisitive eyes of youth. The warm, still air of the night seeped through the room and wrapped around us. To ask any questions of Oscar at this moment would seem an impertinence, but though the hour was late, none of us was ready to end the day. Silent and content, we sipped deliciously cold beer that Joan brought back from Hamjy's rum shop, watching the shadows dancing in the orange glow of the oil lamps. Suddenly Oscar gave a start and

* Locally distilled rum, also called Jom's toddy or *cumfia*.

announced that there was a party tonight in Old Town, and would we care to shake a leg?

Old Town was about a twenty-minute walk along the beach; we walked slowly and in silence. It was a strange feeling to go out into the night and find the air warmer outdoors than indoors. As we walked along the beach, the acrid smell of rotting seaweed cut through the hanging scent of frangipani. Tiny waves lapped against rocks and pebbles in accompaniment to the soft pad of our footsteps on the wet sand. We passed the dark silhouettes of houses dimly lit inside by a flickering flame. The inhabitants sat in doorways, heads resting on hands, elbows on knees, chatting softly or humming to the strum of a guitar. Even the dogs were still, resting from their never-ending round of foraging and fighting.

As we drew near Old Town we could hear the throbbing of the guitars, muffled in the night, and the sputter of maracas accompanying an inaudible tune. The faint lamplights punctured the darkness of the village, and we turned off the beach to follow the path that brought us nearer the music. The party was in a small house that stood high off the ground. Underneath the house small groups of people stood around looking at each other. The rickety dwelling shook to the stamp of feet beating out the rhythm of the dance, and in the cold, surgical light of a Petromax lantern, we could see a surging mass of people heaving through the room. Oscar said we should go in, so we climbed the broken-down ladder and stood in the doorway. Inside, the room was thick with smoke and sweat, and the heat could almost be seen in the hard lamplight. Over in one corner sat the band, four boys between twelve and eighteen years old: two played guitars and another an accordion;

the fourth held the jawbone of a horse and vibrated it for the rhythm. That was what I had thought to be maracas. The boys sat hunched over their instruments, blank, unfeeling expressions on their faces—a strange contradiction to the exciting pulse of their music. Between tunes they passed around a bottle of rum.

When she saw us in the doorway, the hostess of the party threaded her way through the dancers, welcomed us, and led us to another corner where some of the elder men of the village were standing. The hostess was also the island nurse, and she was giving this party for a profit. Everyone paid two pesos to come in, and she sold the drinks and the cakes. She was an enterprising woman who found many ways to make money. We took our drinks and ate our cakes. Meanwhile Oscar had made his way to another corner where he ate, drank and smoked his cigarette. With some prodding from the hostess and her friends, Joan and I took a turn at dancing, and when he saw us, Oscar shook his leg and laughed. The small children scattered around the room laughed at Oscar's gesture; they started to tease him a little. He told them they should have respect for their elders and betters, and asked, "Did your mammy teach you no manners?" Then, while the band took a breather, others in the room began to tease Oscar, but it was all in fun and he enjoyed being the center of attention. They asked him to sing a song and he obliged. Closing his eyes and striking a pose that suggested Napoleon ordering his army to charge, he boomed out a song called "Beans," which may or may not have had a tune and which seemed to have many different tempos. I could not make out the words to the whole song, but the first stanza (and there seemed to be at least twenty) went roughly as follows:

> BEANS, beans, BEANS, beans,
> Beans for the judge,
> Beans for the jury,
> Beans for the lawyer,
> Beans for the guilty,
> For all that them say
> And them say a plenty,
> The answer is beans,
> Beans times twenty
> BEANS, beans, BEANS, beans, beans!

Everyone laughed while Oscar sang the song; when at last he finished, they all applauded, saying "Oscar is a joke man!" and gave him a drink. Flushed with his success and with the rum, Oscar moved out into the center of the room and recited the following poem:

> You call me sweet and tender names,
> And softly soothe my tresses,
> But all the while my happy heart
> Beats time to your caresses.
>
> I love you in my gentle way
> And answer as you let me,
> But oh! I only dread the day,
> The day when you forget me.
>
> Your hearts are fickle, I know it well
> There'll come a day when we must sever,
> Yet my love for you will always dwell,
> And remains with you forever.

Yea, hush my whisper as you may,
Your chidings cannot fret me.
But oh! I only dread the day,
The day when you forget me.

I know your ever-beating heart
Still marks the thought I bring you;
I know there dwells a noble power
In the sweet songs I sing you.

Yea! Hush my whispers as ye may
Your chidings cannot fret me.
But oh! I only dread the day,
The day when you forget me.

"God bless all broken homes, Amen!" He was thinking of his own.

Everyone thought it was a beautiful poem, and their subdued air testified to its effect. One of the girls took Oscar a drink, handing it to him with a slight involuntary curtsy of respect. He took the drink and swallowed the stinging rum in one gulp, as if to chase away the sadness he had brought upon himself. Everyone else took time out for a drink and other refreshments, and then the band started to play again. Oscar was no longer in the mood for such gaiety; he asked if we were ready to go home. The memories racing through his mind showed up as sadness in his eyes. He wanted to talk more, to relieve himself of the torture of his thoughts by getting them outside of himself. It was very late, and the hour, the heat and the rum had pretty well readied me for sleep, but Oscar's need was more urgent.

We said our thank-yous, explained our tiredness and wished everyone a good night and a good party. Our hostess said she had been honored by our coming and hoped we would come again, "any time."

We walked slowly along the beach until we came to the small memorial to Rojas Pinilla, the former dictator of Colombia. The bust of Rojas had long since been toppled, so all that remained was the pedestal standing in the middle of a walled-in square which included, in one corner, the remains of a basketball court. Oscar sat on the low wall, placed his chin in his hands and stared at the dark sea. Joan silently continued on her way, and I sat down beside Oscar.

"I was married at an early age in the year 1919, around nineteen years. My wife, Mrs. Rafaela Newball de Bryan, had poor aspiration. I married because she had trapped me. She had notions to become a coquette, and I was too tender to foresee the end of the trail. We fell apart after eight years, and for thirty-five years I have bewailed my gain and my loss. To this union are born five children, but we all fell apart, and until this day they are lost to the wolves of society. My days are few and troublesome, but God has helped me and may help me to endure to the last. For this I am grateful. God bless my broken home. May He superintend. From the hand of the omnipotent One, may nothing be lost, for there is never a day the sun has never shine: the trouble is with our vision.

"My son Oswald was bent on straying. At the age of twelve my uncle enticed him, at whose charm he renounced his father, and for that he became a wanderer to this day. His last letter of August 25, 1960, told of his plight, sick and broken and not recognized. This tore up my sad heart. The son of my choice, whose eventful name is the power of God, is now a wanderer, lost and straying, probably bumped off. Oh, God! Is a broken home not the only hell below? How can a Christian afford all this!

"My daughter Lacy is laid in the jungles of those Indians that join pirate Morgan in his loots. May God watch over her grave and have mercy on her soul.

"My son Hugh, he is trying, but is infested with tuberculosis, whose germs the Red Cross succeeded to drug. May God bless him, because of the humiliation of his dad, not able to care for that which is committed to his hand.

"My daughter Clarissa, she also wanders. Wandered away. She seems to have lost parental sympathy and for years has forgotten the father who has tenderly cared and fought many battles with her mother, who had neither foresight nor heart. God bless her. May heaven preserve her and wave her banners forever over her.

"My son José awaits the resurrection of the dead. If not the first, the second will tell. He became the jeers of his simple-minded uncles and aunts, who nicknamed him 'String Beans.' But to his daddy he is the sum of his loss, anguish and remorse. Today, I am a broken man more or less, far or less, childless, wifeless, and with nothing to live for except the reflection of the past. But courage makes the man. If the Almighty Banners wave over him, God bless my enemies. Those who oppose themselves for their sins remain and shall remain as long as eternity lasts. For they are concealed sins, they need not confess, for the time is now past.

"It is now thirty-five years since she has left me.

She was hellish when she was young, but you change as you grow. It is bad if you have culture and your wife does not. It is a misfit. During our eight years of marriage I did everything to educate her I could think of, but that was not her ambition. She was after men. I could not exchange ideas with her or reason with her. My conception of woman is that she has to have the capacity for growth. But she has broke my career.

"In a broken home, it is not you that suffer as much as the children, but they had me tied down before I could give them preparations. Today you have to have preparation for the world. My sin is the sin of neglect. Now I have left my home and become a doormat for my countrymen."

Now it was all out in the open. The hopes that he might be able to compensate for an incomplete childhood home were finally destroyed by the breakup of his marriage. The ambition to be the father to his children that his father had never been to him was finally frustrated. The desire for a wife who could mirror and applaud his intellectual attainments, who could encourage him in his mission and have faith in his rightness, was totally unfulfilled. Instead, his wife "broke" his career and Oscar was left stranded, isolated, a "doormat" for his countrymen.

In the beginning those responsible for him—his parents and his brethren—failed. But that was not his fault. Then came his chance, the time when the responsibility was his, when he made the choice. And he failed. He chose the wrong woman for a wife, and he could not live up to his own ideal for himself as a father to his children. When they needed him, he could not go to them, and now they did not even know him.

At this point he had become detached from the mainland and was now the island that no man is. Hunched up by the wall, he sat silent and alone, complete in himself. Yet he had needed me. Perhaps he was not so complete after all; perhaps there was still a bridge to the mainland.

He took a cake from his hat and bit into it. The first gray and pink strokes of dawn brushed across the night sky. Suddenly we were startled out of our silence by the piercing honk of the conch shell, a sound like that of a terror-stricken cow. This meant that a boat had come through the reef and was rounding Lookout Hill. It would be the *Contessa*, one of Jenkins's boats, which had been expected for the past couple of days.

As we sat there on the wall, we watched tousled heads poke sleepily through the shutters, aroused by the conch's blast. Doors opened to let half-naked infants out to pee in the yard, followed by the drowsy adults making their way to squat on the beach. With much stretching and grunting, the morning began. Little boys and girls filled buckets of water from cisterns or barrels; rumpled women, their torn dresses hanging half on and half off, lit the fires with much blowing and cursing; the men, after initially rising, sat down again to wait for coffee while they scratched heads, armpits and stomachs. Smoke from the fires began to curl up through the roofs or out through the slatted kitchen windows. Coffee or bush tea was soon bubbling and the leftovers from the day before were heating up.

We just sat. The *Contessa* appeared around the point, looking not much bigger than a rowboat, squat and flat in the water. Slowly she reached the center of the bay and dropped anchor. We could barely see the tiny shapes of people moving around her deck, watching the island's early-morning preparations. When she dropped anchor, Oscar arose and said he must go out to inspect her. He went off down the beach, pushed a canoe out onto the water, and was paddling off before the owner realized what had happened.

I got up and walked slowly back home to wash and somehow or other compensate for the loss of a night's sleep. All around there was much activity as people made their various preparations for the arrival of the boat.

After a wash and several cups of restorative coffee, I went down to the small concrete wharf at the side of Jenkins's store to watch the comings and goings as the *Contessa* disgorged its surprises. I arrived just in time to see Oscar reach land with a most extraordinary passenger.

His name was Vidor the Vagabond. Everything about him was striking. He was a large man but his most striking feature was a big, bushy, golden-gray beard curling out from his face in all directions. Above the beard protruded a large, but not too large, bulbous, but not too bulbous, nose; atop that were two piercing gray eyes. On his head he wore a wide-brimmed straw hat without a crown. His long gray hair was tied in a top knot that bobbed, Sikh fashion, above the straw rim. Around his neck he wore several necklaces, one made of animals' teeth, another of bird beaks, and another of seeds. A battered camera swung like a talisman across his middle, and the large pockets of his voluminous black coat bulged with unidentified objects. He wore enormous baggy pants (something like a circus clown's pants) and had a pair of rubber boots on his feet.

He got out of the canoe and then hauled up a large gray canvas knapsack, which he slung on his back, and a black umbrella. Oscar followed him out of the canoe and tied it to a post. Vidor the Vagabond complained of hunger and gave Oscar some money to go and buy bread, which he did.

Meanwhile, Vidor was quickly surrounded by a crowd of curious islanders, which explained why he did not notice me. He asked them to let him through, but he and they moved like a phalanx off the wharf, up the street and onto the nearest stretch of beach. Here Vidor the Vagabond took a hammock from his knapsack, strung it between two palm trees, climbed in it and slowly swung his great bulk back and forth.

Oscar came back with two loaves of bread. Vidor said he asked for only one and that Oscar should take the second one back and return him the change. Oscar said he would do no such thing, but would eat the second loaf for his pains. Still swinging calmly, Vidor called Oscar a beggar. "I know your sort," he continued. "You can't fool me."

"If that is how ye repay the hospitality of the island," Oscar retorted, "then climb back on board and go back whence ye came." For the rest of Vidor's stay on the island, Oscar and he did not speak to each other.

Oscar left the crowd and Vidor began to speak to some of them. He began by telling of his travels. He had traveled all over the world—Jamaica, Tahiti ("Ever heard of Tahiti?" he asked), Africa, Hong Kong, Samoa, the Canaries. He spoke in a soft, gentle, yet patronizing tone of voice. In fact, when he discovered that islanders understood English perfectly well (it was, after all, their native language), he began to intersperse his conversation with Spanish phrases meant to impress them. At random he would ask a bystander questions: about sex ("Do you fuck girls or old women?" he asked of one young man); about their ambitions ("And what do you want to do with your life, fry in the sun?"); about their achievements ("What did *you* learn in school, huh?"). Then he told them they were lazy and good for nothing but rum and whores.

It was not for quite a while that he noticed me standing at the back of the crowd. When he finally did, he was so startled he leaped out of his hammock, introduced himself and asked who I was. I invited him back to the house and he gladly accepted my invitation.

Vidor the Vagabond had been traveling the world for thirteen years, living by his wits. He said he was from the smallest republic in the world, San Marino, and that his grandfather, Sir Antony, had written the famous book about the republic. He himself was "a crown prince sort of thing"—and he casually waved his hand. He had grown up in the United States, always hearing tales of the exploits of his world-traveling ancestors, and his nanny had been a woman from Providencia.

He studied at Columbia University in New York; there he became interested in sociology and the Negro. One question above all raised itself in his mind: Why was it that of all the races in the world, Chinese, Indian and white, the Negro had never managed to build a civilization?

To answer this question he had decided to visit every part of the world where Negroes lived. He lived with them in their homes and their doss houses; he talked and drank, slept and argued with them for thirteen years. To pay for his travels, he would set up a small village school, teaching arithmetic, English, reading and writing; train a village teacher or two; and then sell the school to the village. He would accept any marketable commodity in payment. He had sold a school for five thousand coconuts, for elephant tusks, for pepper and cloves, for fifty cows. Whatever he got, he would somehow market where there was a demand for that item. But now he was on the last leg of his travels and would soon return to San Marino to become the first professor of sociology at the university there. As a result of his extensive research, he had also found the answer to his question.

"It is simple," he said. "Old women rule the Negro race. Go anywhere they live and you will find the young men living off the old women. She feeds them and gives them a place to sleep. She gives them a girl too, but they have to sleep with her in return. You see, Negro women are sexually more intense and remain sexually active for far longer than other women. They simply wear out the men, so they must have a supply of young men about them. They make the money and support the men, and that's all right with the men because it means they don't have to work. So the men have neither the strength nor the inclination to devote themselves to the work and the creativity that would build a civilization. Go where you will, and you will find they are all beggars. On this island you will find it is the same story. Just give me a few days and I will show you."

He was never able to convince me that his theory applied to Providencia, though a few days later he assured me that "everyone fucked their grandmothers," though "not as much here as in some of the other places he had been." Nevertheless, Vidor's palmistry and his medicines quickly became known throughout the island. He specialized in divining the problems of love and infidelity and offering solutions for them. He lacked no customers during his stay, and I have no doubt of his claim to have made enough money to pay for his visit.

He and Oscar avoided each other completely. Each apparently felt that he had met his match, when he had thought he was matchless!

After a ten-day stay, Vidor the Vagabond left the island, taking with him a horse, which he said he would sell in Panama at a great profit. He was in every sense a large man in a small world and I do not doubt that he is still wandering and listening to the variations in other men's themes.

While Vidor was with us we saw nothing of Oscar, but comparisons were inevitable. Here in the person of Vidor the Vagabond was a classic figure: the Wanderer embarked on the Quest, and as singular in his way as Oscar. Yet why did Oscar choose to avoid the man? Certainly their initial misunderstanding did not help, but one would have thought that in his desire to meet with his equals, even his superiors, in learning, Oscar might have taken advantage of Vidor's presence. After all, the reason he had been drawn to me in the first place was because I am an educator, a "professor." Oscar never referred to Vidor except to say once that he was a man of some learning and little insight.

The clue, perhaps, is in this single observation. Like Elder Sigmund, Vidor had only learning and no wisdom. The Grand Quest reveals itself as a lie, an illusion tricked out with science—"counterfeit science," as Oscar calls it. Why did the Negro never build a civilization? Not only is the question based on false assumption, but even if it were a valid one, it could never be answered. Thirteen years of travel, experience, ingenuity, theory and accumulation of knowledge were all founded on a vast irrelevancy. And the racist arrogance of the man was painful to Oscar, and embarrassing to me. But this suggested that his vast search into others' inadequacies was but a monumental effort to deny his own.

Which way does madness lie, I wonder?

It was just coming into cane-grinding time, Oscar's favorite time of the year.

Cane-grinding on the island presented a chance for great liberation. Time was reversed. Everyone stayed up through the night and took long siestas during the day.

In one corner of a field the women sat over a fire, stewing fruits in the thick molasses—oranges, pine-apple, papaya, tamarinds, coconuts—popping bits and pieces into their mouths and into the mouths of the children. They laughed and gossiped through the night. Nearby another fire was sunk into the ground, tended by the "boiler." Huge black vats with bubbling cane juice slowly thickening to molasses rested precariously over the fire, and the boiler kept the fire going and stirred the syrup. In the middle of the field was the mill—four rollers set vertically and turned by black greasy cogs, worked in turn by four helicopter-style blades attached to one or two horses being driven around in circles by small boys. The cane stalks were fed into the rollers and the juice bubbled frothy white down a chute into a bucket. After each bucket was full, someone, usually a small boy, would dip a coconut in and swig, then take the bucket over to the boiler, who would pour it into the vats. Little boys would jump on and off the horses' backs, chase each other around the mill, and fight and play tag in the mound of pressed cane stalks. Men sat around the field drinking rum, talking, playing dominoes, taking turns supervising the mill or just stretching out in the moonlight. The young men would strum guitars, drink rum and slink off with the girls, and now and again a couple would dance. It was a time when everyone was free to relax in public, when the fronts of everyday life could be taken down without fear.

It was during this time that Oscar could be free with the rest of the island, and he worked indefatigably night after night. He was an especially good boiler, knowing exactly how hot to make and keep the fire, and exactly how to control the consistency of the syrup. Like anyone else who worked at cane grinding he was paid in kind, and he was able to sell the syrup he received and enjoy more prosperity than at any other time of the year. Most of the syrup boiled on the island went to distillers, but Oscar refused to sell to them because, he said, they polluted the product. During the two weeks or so when cane grinding was at its height we hardly ever saw Oscar except when he was passing through on his way to another cane grind; then he would stop by briefly and give us a can of freshly boiled syrup, and perhaps some candied fruit.

Then as the moon waned and most of the cane stalks had been ground, the night returned to night and the day to day, people returned to their houses and their shut-in lives, and Oscar was left alone out in the open. That was when he returned to us. After all the excitement and hard work of the past couple of weeks, he looked very tired and strained, and something seemed to have upset him. It turned out that a friend of his, Elijah Archbold, had died over in Southwest Bay. Oscar claimed Elijah had died as a result of obeah, for he had "had a contention with Lanswell Hoy over a pack of cigarettes and a stolen camera."

I asked Oscar how this could have led to Elijah's death.

"Oh! Many ways of hanging a dog as well as by the neck," he answered. "You have sciences genuine and counterfeit, and obeah is a counterfeit science."

"Tell me about obeah," I said.

"This science has been brought to life by the Fox girl of Rochester, New York, in the year 1848. The mysterious rapping gave us the formula and the key for it—the bill and the receipt. These are the sciences of the sixth and seventh book of Moses and the Book of the Black Arts, and are in Article Ninety-nine of the British Police Code. Mysterious arts that are some of the discoveries of the civilized lands. They hand them down, but some of these things is not for the general public—what a mess we'd have. You can see through that; without that we'd have such a mess. Suppose they were to know some of the things that some of us know. But you say except you know these things you are not yet instructed. Yes, these are mysterious arts. Better that for them education is knowing genealogy, Jewish law, poetry, and music.

"We are watching with keen interest the development of this science after which the inhabitants of Old Providence and Saint Andrews now seek—the coming science: obeah. But obeah is the science after which all the civilized nations seek. Even churches practice it, thus bringing to pass the predictions of the noted Englishman—is he Sir Walter Raleigh? I'll have to be straight on that. I like to be accurate. Spiritualism is the coming science. Yes, we are watching with keen interest the development of this science after which the inhabitants of these islands now seek."

"Oscar, how does this obeah work?" I asked.

"It works if you are not able to get off obeah in time. You hear like a scapegoat under the Jewish economy bearing the sins of the people for one year. The Day of Atonement, those sins collected in the sanctuary three hundred and fifty-nine days were on the last day of the year confessed, or taken as a symbol upon himself by the priest to cleanse the sanctuary. The priest confesses these sins taken upon himself upon the head of the scapegoat. The scapegoat is led into the wilderness by a fit hand to perish as a symbol that Satan, or the Devil, the originator of a mysterious science known as mesmerism or hypnotism, who used a serpent to beguile our first mother Eve. They used the serpent as a medium who beguiled mother Eve. The serpent talked. Since then the more civilized nations have more keenly perfected the art.

"The obeah man of Old Providence Island is supposed to be Barnaby Britton. Oliver Archbold, who is getting to be a desperate character, posing as a minister. He has a special malice against me. We went to the same school. He took a ten-week session, I had nine months, so he expected to be a man of my capacity. Lots of his proceedings are work up by schemes of his—deceit and fraud. He is now in the service of the Jenkins, who are able robbers of national funds and noted contrabanders. Their medium is Elder Ricardo Jenkins, who had been graduated in the West Caribbean Training School, Canal Zone, as a preacher. Ay, the same that ranted this weeks past in Rocky Point.

"A noted man of these parts, Cyrus Dawkin of Old Town, seems to have been versed in the science, introduced to us from Bocas del Toro. He took Ilma Forbes of Old Town, who was suffering presumably from the symptoms of obeah, to the graveyard. He told her to sit down and under no consideration may you run. Who he called up in his incantation he demanded a fingernail. A fight ensued between Cyrus and the ghost, but in the battle Cyrus lost his fingernail. Forbes was given five black stones to burn every Friday, and the Friday that Forbes did not burn these stones, the ghost gave her hell. The wife of the teacher Rafael Archbold had a keen impression that this fingernail could be condensed into powder and Forbes wear it around her neck as a guard, like some mothers put around their babies' neck a guard—a little bag with string and red powder.

"Mr. Oscar Bryan, known as Professor Oscar Newball of these parts, is still among us in the land of the living by the kindness of the God of Jacob, Isaac and Abraham or his bones would have been white before now and eaten for their phosphorous. Professor Newball can burn the candle at both ends. He prays on bended knees, both of them, and his mother's God has respect to his position, but his wife, seeing how sadly she failed in her expectations, is now afraid of Oscar Bryan for thirty-five years since she became an estranged wife. Plenty for obeah.

"There is an adage—bad luck is worse than obeah. You may cure obeah, but no scientist is capable of curing bad luck, for without God nothing may be done."

Letting himself go on the forbidden subject of obeah seemed to smooth some of the lines of strain from Oscar's face, and he told these things with relish, almost perhaps with a spite against his fellow islanders. After all, it was their madness that they had to resort to obeah, and toward this Oscar felt very superior. He asked for some fever-grass tea, which we all drank liberally laced with cane syrup. The warm sweet tea set him going again, and I switched on the tape recorder.

"All like this Captain Gidalty Bryan, who has been master of many vessels, bought a guard for sixty pesos. The Captain believed had it not been for that, his bones would have been white long ago for the job.

"The Captain live out his threescore years and ten plus. He died in contention with Ferdy Bryan and his uncle Wedna Bryan over a sow that Ferdy had maliciously chopped up and killed. The municipal judge found Ferdy guilty, and he was put in prison for two months in the Police Station at Nelly Downs and he was sentenced to pay for the sow one hundred and eighty-five pesos—which his brother Selsus Bryan put up, that Ferdy might be free from the strong arms of the law. It is reported that Wedna Bryan and his wife Casilda Archbold de Bryan had employed John Thomas, a noted brouhaha of these parts and Santa Isabel, who had studied with Dr. Titch Jay (a noted scientist and

Peter J. Wilson

medical man) that if something is not done it is because John Thomas does not know anything.

"Mr. John Thomas is a confederate of Captain John Jenkins. The brain of his science comes from the upstairs pavilion of the Captain John Jenkins, who is a notable character on both land and sea of these parts. When he tells John the confederate to charge for a case fifty pesos, five pesos looks like plenty of money to John. Thus they disagree. John Thomas has taken on the responsibility for the deaths of Napoleon Newball of Old Town and Captain Alston Bryan of Rocky Point, who had lived some years in Colorado Bay, Bluefields and Nicaragua.

"When Captain Gidalty Bryan died, Professor Oscar Bryan came down to Town Bay and advised Mr. Thomas and his confederate who may implicate; the Judge ask to take on Captain Gidalty Bryan. But he, Professor Oscar Bryan, is the avenger of the blood of his brother, and if John had pissed in the President's drink, he would have been better off for it.

"John is now laid in the cemetery at Captain Sheridan Archbold, on the other side awaiting his life-giver, the minister of second death, which shall be paid with fire. Professor Oscar Bryan Newball still has much confidence in his mother's God and his father's Christ, who present his cause continually before the Most High Judge, who is God Himself. Obeah has taken its toll. Obeah men are getting despondent, for lots of them can kill, but can't cure.

"The more ignorant a man, the less God want as to do with him because He cannot tolerate a fool. Sometimes man is making an ostentation show, a great brag, but when you bring him to the test he has to take to the background. Ignorance is more deadly than war."

It was a good line on which to end, and Oscar knew this very well. After we drank a nightcap, Oscar laid out his latest belongings on the porch, and then settled down to sleep. Next morning he was gone.

By this time we were never really sorry when Oscar was not around, although for the most part we still enjoyed his company. But by now we had been on the island for a while and were beginning to feel claustrophobic, shut in by the limitless sea and by the selves we had to constantly assume, for we always had to appear friendly, sympathetic and willing to listen, no matter what our mood.

Sometimes when Oscar was away, Seferino would come around. A tiny, hunched-up alcoholic, he would totter shakily into the room and with a soft, purring voice ask us if we did not wish to buy some land, which he would love to sell us. Or perhaps we would like some limes that he had just picked, or if we did not want either, why didn't we just give him an advance on the day when we did want land or limes? Well, if we had no cash, a cigarette would do, and once he had his cigarette he would stagger off, blessing us and promising us the whole island.

If it was not Seferino, it might be Larwell. A hulking, square-shouldered man with only two teeth in his head, and those more like fangs, he would holler from halfway up the path, "Ho! Mr. Pete." At least it was fair warning. Then there would follow a long story about how he and Garcia were going fishing and this would mean they would soon have plenty of money, but in the meantime they had none, and could I lend him some?

Or it was Rexford. A powerful, handsome man, son of the famed Captain Ellsworth, Rexford was a man desperately trying to hold on to himself but day by day feeling his hold slipping. Drunk and slobbering, he would stop by and ask for money for more to drink. Then the next day he would come back quite sober, his eyes full of tears, to apologize remorsefully for his behavior of the night before, and pay back the money he had borrowed.

We had an invitation to spend a few days with Captain Ellsworth, who lived around the island in Lazy Hill, so one day we saddled the horses, packed a change of clothes, and set off along the beach through Old Town toward Lazy Hill. There was no one on the beach but a few little children splashing in and out of the water and some chickens running and pecking. As we passed by each house along the way, heads would pop up at the windows to ask where we were going and to relay the information back into the darkness.

Unlike the other villages on the island, most of Lazy Hill's houses are located well off the road. As we came to the first house, we had to turn off the road and ride through backyards and up a small hill until we finally arrived at Ellsworth's house, which stood on piles high above the ground. We got there in time for a late lunch of boiled yams and beans and some homemade cassava cake, which we ate underneath the house where they had been cooked. Captain Ellsworth took me up to the verandah, where we sat rocking lazily to and fro, and Joan went off with the Captain's daughter Lilith, her particular friend.

Lilith radiated softness, although she was a large, rather clumsily built woman. She played the guitar as though her fingers never really touched the strings, and she sang in a voice of childlike sweetness and simplicity. But most striking of all was her immense sensitivity toward people. Though she'd had very little schooling and had left the island only once—then to go only as far as San Andrés—she seemed to understand and sense the emotions and personalities of other people so intensely that she could communicate with anyone. She and Joan were able to relate to each other as friends who could genuinely love each other, although there were all the differences in the world between them.

Captain Ellsworth was a huge man. He claimed that at one time he had weighed nearly four hundred pounds, but that now since he had been dieting, he managed to keep his weight steady at some point well over three hundred pounds. He was fierce-looking, his appearance suited to his reputation as having been the most feared captain of his day, and his bulging build was made all the more awesome by the intense blackness of his skin, a blackness that seemed nearer to a deep purple. His large eyes appeared to flash from their deep sockets and clasp the listeners' attention in their gaze. Yet when he spoke it was in a soft, light voice that rarely rose above a whisper. He was now well into his sixties, but the only evidence of advancing age was a few gray hairs. After almost fifty years at sea he had retired "to devote his life to farming and to God." For after his wild life at sea he had become a convert to Seventh-Day Adventism and was intent on living to the letter the demands of that creed. He still spoke with pride of some of his exploits—how he had once defeated six men single-handedly, how he'd evaded coastal patrols and outwitted the authorities during his smuggling career. He was especially proud of his method of smuggling whiskey in coconuts. This he did by boring a hole in the coconut with a fine glass drill and draining out all the coconut milk. Then he pumped the Scotch in with a syringe, sealed up the minute hole and took his shipment of coconuts to Cartagena or Panama. Here it was unloaded, put on a truck, and taken by devious routes to a secret bottling plant, where the Scotch was decanted, watered down, and put into bottles with various expensive labels that were popular in the night clubs. Then they were trucked up to Bogotá or reexported to Panama, and sold at seven times the price. Captain Ellsworth was also proud of his special mention as a "fierce buck Negro" in a *Reader's Digest* article that described the activities of various islanders who had been involved in helping Germans during the last war. He was better known by the title Cap'n Nigger.

Now he had given up his rough ways and his drinking and had insisted that his wife and daughter follow his religion, too. But he could not control his son Rexford, who like his father was a licensed sea captain and enjoyed the rough life. Though his father condemned him, it was a hollow condemnation, for he really felt that a young man should believe in a young man's religion, and he was now an old man. Months later, long after we had left the island, Lilith wrote and told us that Rexford had been killed while he was skippering a boat smuggling she knew not what, between Panama and the Guajira.

There we sat watching the afternoon sun slowly begin its descent below the sea, rocking to and fro, the big Captain swigging away at a bottle of soda which he took from a kerosene refrigerator crammed full of bottles. After a while the conversation turned to Oscar, for the Captain and Oscar had long been good friends.

"I advise you never to be afraid of Oscar, or if you be then never to let him know it; otherwise he will plague you. Them say he is mad, but once they was to take him to Bogotá to be examine and he were gone for two years. No one seem to know what happen but when the Director see him, he say to Oscar, 'The people as sent you here is more mad than you.' Certain it is there is something wrong with him, like he were crazy some of the time. Him use to make this place his home for a couple of year. I gave him some odd jobs to do and pay him a couple of peso. He bring me fish and fruit but when I take out the peso he say, 'As long as you're feeding me, you don't pay.' Oscar is the best fisherman I ever see. Him can catch a barracuda right close in at the shore. One time he come and say to borrow a hook and line. He came back in a short time and say a fish has taken the hook and to please lend him another one. He came back this time and a large snapper he catch in the mouth of Salt Creek. Sometimes he borrow money too, like a ten peso, but he always pay you back, even it were ten years later.

"One time him and me has a quarrel. My wife is from Grand Cayman and is a British subject. One day, Oscar come in in a joke and say, 'We must get rid of the foreigner.' He had come up to the house to get fish for a woman in Southwest Bay and him think that I leave the house already. But I is in the bedroom dressing. So when him come in and say, 'We must get rid of the foreigner,' I come out into the room to surprise and joke him. Oscar had a machete in his hand and he raised it to me, so I grab a broom and give him a wallop. Oscar run from the house and across the garden yelling like his lungs burst! Someone ask him if he get a fish. Oscar say, 'No!' He got no fish, but he got a wallop!"

The big captain was shaking with laughter as he told the story. "Oscar never come around this place again for three years, although I bear him no grudge. But finally he ask me to take him around to Town in my boat, and we is friends again."

"I tell you another story about Oscar. One day I ask him to chop down some bush for me. I agreed to pay him. But after him cut down the bush he begin to cut down the trees as well. I tell him he was not able to do that, and he say he was letting in the air. But I threaten him and tell him he is not to cut down trees. So Oscar climb the tree to sulk and him would not come down from the tree till nightfall!"

While the Captain was talking, Watler Bush, his neighbor and friend, had joined us. After pulling up a chair on the verandah, and pouring himself a soda, he added his views on Oscar.

"Oscar is very intelligent, you know, and it is difficult to say just what is wrong with him. Sometime he is well for a year or more. Then nobody see him except when he comes around to apologize for all that he done. A few years ago him is sent to Bogotá to be examined in the hospital, but when he get there he is quite sane. In fact he is a very good cobbler and when he is in, he make and fit a good boot. He has some land which he farm pretty well too. And so when him is in, he live most like anyone else. But then sudden-like he go mad. There is no sign. He takes off his shoes and he begins to wander. And when he is mad, he begin to steal things. All like him steal the washing from off the clothesline and distribute it in everyone else's yard. He say he is taking things to keep them in a safe place, but you can always tell when he has taken anything because he leaves something for an exchange—a piece of cigarette, a shell, a coconut or a piece of wood.

"He once took the records from the Treasury Office and hid them in a garbage can. Most naturally everyone know him have done it. The police accuse him, but he deny it. I suggest that the police ask him to help them find the records. When they ask him, he agree to help them if they make him a detective. But he would not help them if there was someone else around. As soon as they went, most naturally he found the records and returned them! Then he ask for his reward.

"What is more entertaining is when he set up a pulpit in the square in Town and preach a sermon. It frequently last for an hour or more, and it is most excellent. Him make a lot of sense and make a lot of quotations from the Bible which is very accurate. But he also mention the people of the island by name and tell how they behave, or perhaps misbehave. He recite all he know about their bad deeds.

"At one time him use to lie underneath the houses all the night, and sometime in the day as well, just listening so him know all that is going on inside! And oh! That is plenty, man!" We all rocked with laughter at this.

"And he remember all this. Stores it all up. Yet

even though he vex you a lot of the time, you can't help to be fond of Oscar. There is a lot of people as is afraid of him, but there is no real cause."

I asked Watler if he was afraid of Oscar, but he chuckled and said there was nothing and no one he was "feared of." He paused for a moment, and then continued, "But when Oscar go out, it is like the Devil grasp him, and I suppose I does have a fear of the Devil."

"Amen," said Captain Ellsworth.

Like everyone else who spoke to me about Oscar, Watler and Captain Ellsworth both expressed a sense of ambivalence and puzzlement, never knowing quite what to make of him. Fear stalks close behind ambivalence, and I wondered why Captain Ellsworth rushed out at Oscar when he knew Oscar was only teasing his wife. He couldn't have mistaken Oscar's voice for that of someone else; it is unmistakable. And how did people feel when the man they had "committed" to a Bogotá asylum returned after two years with a report that said he was saner then those who sent him?

Our discussion of Oscar was interrupted by the call to dinner. After dinner there was to be a dance at the far end of the village, and Lerio Henry was to play the music. Lerio was the finest fiddler on the island and he knew all the old tunes, so I wanted to record him. The Captain would not let Lilith accompany us to the dance in spite of our pleadings and assurances, so we went with Watler and Rexford.

In a flimsy thatch lean-to a few dancers were shuffling around to Lerio's spirited music. He was sitting hunched over his violin, playing with a completely abstracted air, his eyes staring straight into space

92

and his bow barely moving over the strings. His music sounded almost as if it came out of the hills of Kentucky or the highlands of Scotland—as indeed it probably did a long time ago. Hearing reels and square dances in the languor of a tropical evening, seeing them danced by ragged Blacks whose bodies swayed to one rhythm, while their shoulders followed another, and their heads and feet still another—all this suddenly hit me as bizarre but at the same time strangely beautiful because ultimately they were so compatible.

We stayed a day or so longer at Lazy Hill, during which time I was mainly concerned with collecting data for the genetic part of my study. Then we bade farewell to our hosts and returned to Town.

Oscar was waiting for us. In fact, he had camped out on our verandah for a couple of days. He asked me if I would go with him to inspect his gardens and fruit trees. He was especially anxious to check his mango trees to make sure that the new crop was not being stolen. That afternoon we set off, and to my surprise we went straight there with no detour, no stopping to see anyone, no picking up objects along the way.

Upon our arrival, Oscar shed his bag and hat and proceeded to shin up the large trees, more like a boy of sixteen than a man of sixty. Sure-footedly he climbed along the boughs, picking what he considered to be the choicest mangoes and throwing them down for me to catch and put in the sack. There are few fruits to equal a mango freshly picked and ripe to perfection. The green skin is blushed with a deep red and leads one to expect the crispness of an apple. The perfume—for such it is—hangs heavy in the air, but is light and tempting in the individual fruit. When we had collected a sackful,

Peter J. Wilson

we sat down beneath the tree and started to peel the thick skin away, revealing the fleshy bright-orange pulp. Sometimes this pulp is stringy, but these had almost the texture of a peach. We ate silently for a long time, soaking ourselves in the juice of the mangoes until our faces and hands were dripping; whatever we used to wipe ourselves dry quickly became saturated and simply wet us the more. I was soon sated, but Oscar could have gone on eating mangoes until nightfall. He ate with gusto, and with much lip-smacking to show how greatly he appreciated the succulent fruit.

Eventually he finished, arose and disappeared for a few minutes into the bush, returning with a calabash of water which we used to rinse the sticky juice off ourselves. Then, with our cigarettes lit, and eyes narrowed looking out over the green hillside down to the sea, I asked Oscar what he thought about the fact that lots of people said he was mad.

He replied, "When mother got old and dim her sight I became the cook. I would become fatty and my wind get short. I would go out on the road and break off the fat; vigorous walks searching this land. For this, my country girls and boys would say he is out again." Chuckles.

"Then they will say I get in. So I am either out or in." More chuckles.

"That is their formula to judge a madman—if he walks, I am mad. If I'm in, he is sane. That is their test tube in madness. If you walk, you are mad; if you are in, you are sane. They call me a madman, but I am proud of this, for there is method in madness and this is my discoveries.

"This people is not foolish, they are cunning and

94

wicked. You see that madness brings us in par: if there were no madness there would be no comparison." Again he chuckled. "They have to make us mad to bring us on a par. Apart from that there would be no comparison. We stand as night and day.

"They can't understand what a cultivated man is like, his capacity, the ability for thoughts. Concentration, that is the road to success. For no inventions are born, we have to develop the art. A king, once inquiring of Euclid if there was no shorter route, was told there is no royal road to Euclid, *you* must develop.

"As madness don't hurt nobody, it don't hurt me, not if there's method in it.

"You see, Professor Oscar Bryan Newball is of the eighth variety, a man of keen insight and wide vision, he may succeed anywhere. His training is too high for the simple-minded, so he always encounter a hard time. But he is learning better how to adapt himself, being a fool with the fools and a fisherman with the fishermen, and in every way he cooperates.

"And so, sir, there are four types of men. The Wise, the Fool, the Simple and the Sleeper, styled in this form: He that knows not, and knows not that he knows not, is a Fool—shun him. He that knows not, and knows that he knows not, is Simple—teach him. He that knows, and knows not that he knows, is Asleep—wake him. But he that knows, and knows that he knows, is Wise—follow him."

With a quiet laugh Oscar bounded to his feet and then climbed the mango tree once again to begin picking replacements for the fruit we had eaten. This took only a few minutes, after which Oscar came down and began eating again, his toothless jaws biting through the soft flesh. Then we lay down and both of us fell asleep. Oscar awoke with a start, saying he had had a dream.

"I seen a woman in a cave of water. This woman has an apparatus on her head, look like she were stifling. She has on red army boots and all the water came down on her head but the shoes were always dry. In her sympathy to try and help her remove the apparatus off her head, I woke up. The apparatus look like some game, some foul play and business."

We laughed over the dream and wondered what it meant. Oscar had never before admitted to having dreams, although I had often asked him.

By now the violet light of the evening was starting to neutralize the colors of the day. We sat up and stretched, and agreed that we should be on our way home. Oscar hefted the sack onto his back, staggering under the weight and bulge of the mangoes within, and we slowly began the walk back to Town. We stopped at every house on the way back. Oscar would bid the occupants of each house a loud "Good evening" and offer them mangoes from his sack. In return, we were sometimes offered refreshments, and since the cane juice had just been boiled, it was usually fruit candied in molasses—sweet, sticky and sickly, but ambrosia to Oscar. We did not reach Town until late that evening, although we walked less than two miles. Oscar did not come up to the house, but bade me good night at the foot of the path and proceeded on to Town, saying he was going to "sanitate" the main street.

That day I had come as close to Oscar as I ever could or would. For much of the time we had been together we had not needed to say anything, though all the time, as Oscar put it, our thoughts were traveling on waves. We had been close at other times: once when we'd gone fishing for the day and another time when we had hiked right over the island, climbing up Peak in the process. Now I realized that the times when we were closest, such as these, were when we were alone, away from all other human presence and in the company of each other and nature. Was this how Oscar managed to maintain his balance? I remembered that the only times he had mentioned being happy were when he could sing songs to the tune of the early morning and the setting sun, and when he was catching his fish. When he took me on these trips, he was allowing me to enter into his real world, where words were not necessary.

Two days later Oscar returned, his right leg bandaged with an old shirt, the dull-red bloodstains indicating the seriousness of the wound. He had been bitten by a dog, he said, although all he had been doing was sanitating a yard. He had treated the wound himself, with herbs, because he had been refused treatment at the clinic. He entered the room and sat in his chair. I offered to bathe the wound and dress it, a suggestion he accepted. This incident reminded him of another time when he had been bitten by a dog. He had made a fuss then and been thrown into jail, but he made such a nuisance of himself that the jailer was only too glad to release him.

With Oscar an invalid and in no charitable mood toward his fellow islanders, there would be ample opportunity to learn more about his life. On other occasions he had dropped hints concerning some of the things he had done, and concerning some of the events that had probably contributed to his illness. It was on these matters that I decided to press him.

"Are you comfortable, Oscar?" I inquired.

"Thank you, Professor, this is the best hospitality I have enjoyed."

"Well, you won't be moving around for a while," I commented, "so while I listen, tell me the secrets of your life."

He began to speak. "At six years of age I joined the Adventist Church of Rocky Point by baptism, and became a member of good and regular standing, diligent of service and strict of eye. I studied with the Elder Sigmund T. Newton, Captain Farquhar Pym, the first Adventist of these parts, and Mr. Xerxes Pym, once *alcalde* of these parts. With Mr. Miguel Forbes, Miss Hannah Taylor—who was very proficient in Spanish— and the Reverend Johnson of Jamaica Island, Father St. John, a Catholic priest undevoted, and many others.

"At an early age I decided to take a change to the mainland. Seeing needs of higher learning I decided to take up studies with the West Caribbean Training School of the Isthmus of Panama Canal Zone, then in the village of Las Cascadas. This is in the year 1923, in which year he took the eighth grade and was graduated with much honor, giving the opening address of said class, the result of much effort.

"He was promoted from a student to the farm superintendent the following year upon the good recommendations of his fellow countrymen. The farm was going a sad way until I took over, then it went from one degree of success to another, cultivating pineapples, bananas, yuccas, sugar cane and a long list of garden stuff. He also introduced the coconut palm that grow and develop creditable on said ground.

"I officiated in this job for four years and then I resign. I had contention with one of the Elders, one Poli, a German, the President of the Panama Conference, who wanted to be Principal. But his ambition were too high for a stranger from so far away. Our contention lay along the lines of finance, for after four years of service they, for lack of foresight and vision, did not see the need of their superintendent existing. So he decided that his first obligation is to his wife, family and children.

"To better his condition and for higher learnings and his ambition to complete his education of the academic studies, he bought a farm in Frijoles. But this did not work out. Then I accepted work of my father-in-law, Sam E. Newton in the Gatun, Spillway Valley. This work was promised to last two years but at the end of three months he is discharged without a minute's notice with his wife impregnant around eight months and his dependent children.

"My father-in-law, he was much like a land shark. They had some schemes, pretending to be a surveyor sometimes, as if this land is divided, so they come and start taking advice from members of the dispute not to be present. Then he would have something to protest, as I was not present. That means the line, the boundary line, can go over again and that means more days for him. Big brains, smart but not clever. Then he finally came to the end and ran on his way. One time he emigrated to the Canal Zone and he said I couldn't live in Providence. He has stirred up so much things and the people is about to stone him. 'I cannot live in Providence.' So he joins hands with one, the Doctor Harry Eino of the Samaritan Hospital, in making a farm in the Gatun Valley because he could not live in Providence. Then he had contention with so much Catholic priest and who not and who not. One Father Turner told him one time, 'From I've been traveling, you are the only black nigger I have ever discern.'

"So he came to the Adventist and wept like a child. Never had a man spoken to him before that way. He wept like a child. Then in his last he died like a dog. That was the finger that led me to Corazel, the mainspring. His son-in-law, his daughter. Envy hell. This was for reasons more than one. My father-in-law was always telling me if it was his consent I could never have had his daughter to wife.

"According to that it looked like I must have deprived him of her then by having impregnated her before the wedding day. That was the envy. He couldn't stand that. He always know about everybody else's daughter and what not, but this one six months in the house and he didn't know it! That was like a moth to his head and his heart. For he get a chance, he struck back. But he was in union with S. T. Newton, my earlier picture friend and his workman, but he always felt I am in his field and that nothing goes straight. I was now ascending in the intellectual higher than Newton— higher than Newton thought I would have gone. I was excelling him who had little time for higher learning. And he couldn't tolerate that. So he saw fit to join hands and extinguish me. And he had friends who were glad of the occasion.

"My father-in-law, nourishing old grudges of eight years ago—for that I took his daughter and he would have had it but she was impregnated—went from office to office advertising the limitations of his son-in-law on the scale of madness. In which the Elder Sigmund T. Newton joined in hand with said Sam E. Newton and became partners in crimes in tripping the professor and extinguishing his family. Many others also join this conspiracy, a conspiracy second to none against a man that was ready to risk everything for the defense of his family and a liberal education.

"They block and trip me, block my progress to have me tripped.

"In my concept I made good until the brethren decided my aspiration is too high for my complexion, and a boy who is scarcely known among his father's sons.

"But now they were trying out a scheme of extinguishing me behind bars and asylum walls. Or it was I was fool enough to believe in drugs. They had drugs, but I had knowledge and fear of God. It was just like the Scriptures saying that when an enemy coming in like a flood against you, the Spirit of the Lord shall lift up a standard against them. But Jesus Christ once said, 'He cometh to me but hath nothing in me.' May I intend 'tis the very experience of our Lord and Savior Jesus Christ? 'Coming to me but hath nothing in me.'

"These headhunters, my father-in-law Sam E. Newton and the Elder S. T. Newton, until today are not capable of acknowledging their crimes or confessing their guilt. They live in a state of concealed iniquity and sin. 'They shall not prosper,' thus saith the Scriptures. 'He that covereth his sins shall not prosper, but whoso confesseth and forsaketh them shall have mercy.' "

Oscar was sitting in his chair with his leg resting on

an upturned box. His face was alive with the strain of the bitter memories that were chasing through his confused mind. Somewhere, many years ago, his mind was breaking, and now he was sitting here twisting and turning a whole life, presenting the past. Was he a sane man confronted by his own insanity or the insanity of others? Was their greed and jealousy real or imagined? Who had been the torturer and who the tortured? There was no doubt that the torture was Oscar's at this moment. There was nothing we could do but to sit and listen, bound like the wedding guests by this Ancient Mariner. Almost without our knowing it the room had grown dark, but no one saw fit to move in order to light the lamps. Oscar's disembodied voice came throbbing out of the blackness of his corner.

"I was confined in the asylum for eight hundred and forty-eight days on the pretense of madness. It was a place where they promoted industry for the insane and feeble-minded. The Doctor said, 'You were a long time in coming here, but we have you now and we will hold you.' The Professor inquired: If he was a long time in coming here, why is he not in the hands of the judges, why the doctors? He told the doctor that day, you have only scourged me in a modern way. His neck has been squeezed six times, hanged, but his God helped him through and he had decided to let eternity reveal the rest. If you couldn't be loved there you had a hard time. Some people have a way of winning their way. A little here and a little there, you know how it is.

"This Corazel Asylum was a home for the aged of the Canal Zone. Then it became used for adverse purposes and for squeezing out their allies. A place of some of the toughs of Panama—they may have even been the stranger. So it had its good and evils.

"It was a place where they promoted industry for the insane and the feeble-minded. A hat industry, carpentry, they had a little wages. I guess they had bigger dividends for the cheap labor. They promoted broom-making and one wife had a better scheme. The training school made a better broom, so she bought two of their brooms and patented it as her broom. I guess that sister look like a pearl in their eyes.

"I lived sometime in a room to myself. Then I was transferred to the mess, a large room upstairs, each one occupy a separate bed. When I went down there I petitioned them for some work to do—for I felt I could master my mind that way. I was their best janitor—then I went to the shop.

"The doctor told me he was going to send me to a better place than Gargas. It was a better place in that you could do a little work, they paid you in cigarettes, some of them packed especially for the asylum. The meals was fine if you were of the type that they could tolerate! But sometimes it was not always the same way. They have a broth that they give you—testing out your strength. I saw an old soldier come in and they begin to tone him on that broth and in fifteen days that robust-looking man was reduced to a skeleton. They tried it on me, but I demanded the oats. They kept me from the oats for eighteen mornings.

"My mother came to the asylum with my little daughter Clarissa, who was afraid of me. The doctors would not let me go back to my island home. They must try out their hellish experiment of extinguishing my life.

However, after three years my brother, Captain Gidalty Bryan, succeeded in appeasing the doctors with a guarantee that I be deported to my island home. An imposition second to none.

"But in that experience of detain eight hundred and forty-eight days the only thing I didn't lose was my soul. I lost my wife. I lost my children. I lost my faith and hope in God. Except my soul. Just my hope in God. I lost everything worthy from this part. And I wasn't suing for that, you see. But I had to pay, and that hurt. Getting something I was meant for. When I had been cultured sufficient to become minister of the Gospel, I thought I was making a man out of myself—I was scarcely a monkey.

"When studying in Panama I also drew my passport, for I am not accustomed to rat passage. When I returned to my island home I wrote back to those headhunters: 'I am back to normal. You ought to be ashamed and throw away your Bibles.'

"While confined in the asylum my wife went into open prostitution, taking one Andrés O'Neill into my home and defiling my marriage bed.

"So I had served the Adventists for twenty years, after which I began to think seriously that the religion of our Lord and Savior Jesus Christ liberates men to harness them behind asylum walls and mash up their families. I took a change of attitude and decided to suffer the government. My training is too high for the simple-minded. See how? I had thought I was making a man out of myself; I was scarcely a monkey."

The bitterness and disappointment were so harrowing that I found it difficult to bear. I could not change the subject, but I tried to get him to talk of the more optimistic memories of his early life. Lighting the lamps and opening cool bottles of beer helped to lighten the mood, I remarked that he was more man than perhaps he took himself to be, and this made him smile and continue his narration.

"I was once a sailor. The compass I learned in half an hour from north back to north and the intercardinal points that fall in between. I sailed the Caribbean from island to coast, but my delight was to go through the Bull's Mouth, the Bocas del Toro. Oh! We had a fruitful trade between Bocas del Toro and Colón, in Panama. We even went up to Almirante selling our fruits, our chickens, our dogs and even cats.

"I became a marine in the thirty-fifth year of this present century on my return from the nation's capital. I sailed through the Boca eight times where river mix with salt ocean water—a very tempestuous outfit.

"I sailed to Santa Marta from Puerto Colombia in six hours. I sailed to the Guajira, to the Cabo Lavella, my destination. But I came back for I came too near to get lost in another. I love the beautiful lakes, the River Magdalena that reach Giradou where tropics and arctic become kindred brothers to warm or chill hearts.

"I lived in Bogotá for ten weeks. My kinsmen try to disarm me, but my brothers were sweet. They give me a barge that repaid my efforts complete. The *Cañonero* was a reservoir to me that shielded me eight years from the sad defeat of my kinsmen, who through reproaches make doormats for our feet.

"Nineteen thirty-five was the time of the Peruvian

struggle when Bellenga Parra* was the goal of our youth. We become volunteers for this, but in failing to reach the frontier I wept. We were towing what was supposed to be a cabin for our soldiers but we could not manage it from Puerto Colombia, so we came back to Cartagena and passed through to the riverbanks to Barranquilla, where she was tied up. This was just about when the war came to an end. The boundaries of Colombia were again defined unmolested until the present day.

"War is sweet if it is for the defense of our country and home. We choose rather to die as a hero than to live in paradise and retreat. God bless our country. May the manna of heaven unite with our daily bread that daily perisheth. God bless our mothers for acting such innumerable parts, producing sons who can take a noble part for the defense of our country, our children and our wives.

"Well, Professor, I guess there is little more to be said. You see how it is. Some for this reason and others for reasons more than one, and yet other for other reasons. We all have our search. I had to associate myself, a man of pomp, ambition and pride, to the ideas of the simple-minded, whose greatest culture is to approach the unfortunate. Now I have lost my confidence in men and Christianity, though not in God. But the Almighty must do something about this thing we call life, and a form of vanity. It has departed from the true sense. We have departed and lost the image of God

* Oscar is probably referring to one of the frequent flare-ups in the border dispute between Colombia and Peru that raged throughout the 1920's and 30's. The issue was finally settled in 1934 when the borders were fixed by mutual agreement.

in our souls. Nothing appeals. The voice of little
children crying for bread? But no. I can't understand it
at all. Now men claim to be made in the image of the
Maker and Creator can yet be this instrument. Something is going on radically wrong in our world.

"When history is history, and the present becomes
the past, this is the darkest picture ever to be painted on
the canvas of time."

Oscar stayed with us for a few days until his leg felt
better. One morning we got up and he was gone.

On New Year's Day, the little square in the middle
of Town was full of gaily dressed people—women in
bright-colored silks and men in crisply starched shirts
and knife-creased khaki pants. From the wide-open
windows of the small Baptist church came the loud,
full-throated singing of the choir, making up in volume
what they lacked in numbers. From the telegraph
officer's little room in the municipal building next to the
church, a radio blared dance music. People stood
around in little groups or strode aimlessly up and down.

Oscar, cradling his hat in the crook of one arm, and
humping his sack over his back, shuffled slowly to the
center of the square. People made way for him. The
singing in the church was stopped, and a sign was given
to turn down the radio. Oscar was about to deliver his
customary sermon for the New Year.

Carefully placing his hat on the stone bench and
his sack on the ground, he took up his stance. Standing
just behind the high back of the bench he rested one
arm on the sill and raised the other one for silence. He
bowed his head, closed his eyes tightly and breathed in
deeply.

"This morning you are dancing the New Year in,

but some of us cannot afford to do that. Do you realize that Death is an enemy, not a friend?

"The only thing, the only thing that can help you is you're a prophet. And we are none of us that. None of us is a prophet. Jesus Christ weeping over Jerusalem that killest the prophet, and those that are sent. Ah! How oft would I have gathered thee as a hen gathers her brood under her wing. But I will not. Behold, the house is left unto desolation, and I was making a survey to see whether Jesus Christ has returned unto that desolate place. I cannot find him. You hear how? I cannot find him.

"For we are come to Hell, for death is an enemy. It decides your destiny for real or woe.

"Ah! These falling leaves here this morning have many lessons to teach. We call them in the yellow-leaf age. Man has the same age, he must fall like that leaf. Wise man would always gang up against a time like that, but like that leaf, they must fall. But not so with a fool. For him, there is no turning back. The people in these parts learn too slowly. They are not sufficiently developed in anything more than cards, booze, dominoes, girls. A true education is not doing ordinary things in extraordinary ways, but doing extraordinary things in ordinary ways. So Jesus Christ commended Mary for having chosen the other way. But the people of this island is too busy to listen. The saying 'Do as I say, but don't do as I do,' doesn't get you anywhere. So I have been advising the deacons of the church that this is the time to pray. All like the Dr. Spurgeon of England who preached what he thought and acted that way, too. He made fourteen thousand converts and England became a better place to live.

"To gang up against God and against anything that looks honorable is to be a Bolshevist. He is the one that tears down. For these lands are very fruitful for the Bolshevists this morning. They tear down everything that look honorable, and they are very fruitful in the isle this morning. The Bolshevists. This island of ours is governed by the Bolshevist Taylors, for do we not see the Administration today is for the Taylor's family. Is it not a Taylor-employed machine? They are marching against God, but death is the enemy and the future is dark.

"The last enemy to be destroyed is death. For the Almighty God is taking this privilege to himself to destroy that last enemy which was introduced here as a foreign element. The wages of sin is death. There are no negative terms in these words. It is an equation for your mathematicians—the wages of sin is death, equals death. But though we may learn death as a way, the gift of God is eternal life, through Christ the Lord.

"The Administration of this island is very dumb, ignorance is no excuse. But the true administration of the Lord through Jesus Christ is an administration in every way. No more an eye for an eye and a teeth for a teeth. This is the administration of hate. A new commandment I give unto you—that you ask one another no more for the administration of hate, for some of us are hate-bound.

"The administration of hate is an eye for an eye and a teeth for a teeth. That is the dispensation of the false, of the moon and of the heartbeat. Where the moon is, there are the heartbeats.

"The administration of the Cross is a dispensation

gone by. This is what you must plan to get back this morning.

"The Jews, mark you, had all Christ and no law. Now we have all law and no Christ.

"Amen, and I thank you."

He picked up his hat and moved his sack over. Slowly he sat down on the stone bench. He took a cigarette from his pocket and lit it; as the blue smoke spiraled up into the sky, he closed his eyes.

An Individual
and
His Society

In my book *Crab Antics* I sought to demonstrate that all Caribbean societies have a dual value orientation which originates in their colonial history, and which persists in their postcolonial situation. Having been dominated and indoctrinated by Euro-American culture, the Caribbean has come to regard this culture, and particularly its values, languages and institutions, as superior to any values originating in its own societies. I called this complex of metropolitan values *respectability*, a term widely used in this sense throughout the English-speaking Caribbean.

Sociologically, respectability is the dogma or charter that supports and authenticates a class structure, and those who are considered respectable are those who are considered upper or middle class. Where they exist, expatriates are arbiters of respectability, but otherwise, and for the most part, the arbiters are natives of the Caribbean. The vast majority of people, however, are not upper class, and are not respectable. This does not mean that the majority live only by negative standards, but rather that there coexists another, indigenous value complex, which—again using a term common in the region—I have called *reputation*.

I have discussed both respectability and reputation, and the relationship between them, in great detail elsewhere, so here I will only summarize what they entail, and briefly indicate their implications.

Respectability is defined through the use and perfection of the language and speech of the metropolitan culture—respectable people speak "proper" English, not creole or patois or bush English. Although it is not mandatory, for respectability a fair skin and Caucasoid facial features are considered highly desirable and aesthetically preferable. But where the aspiring respectable person is not so blessed, then he must maintain a standard of dress and of conduct, and a style of life that are identified with the life of white expatriates or with the metropolis. Dress for men includes shoes, a tie and often a suit, while for women neatness and newness are necessary; manners embrace formal table manners, politeness, obedience by children, and a restrained demeanor. Life style is of course founded on wealth, but wealth alone cannot confer respectability. It is the manner by which wealth is displayed in furnishings, housing and appliances.

Life style and manners have a moral side too, and respectability requires public sincerity in worship at a Christian church, properly married spouses living monogamously in a nuclear family household complete with domestic servants, and a publicly firm observance of sexual propriety (chiefly manifest in the strict chaperonage of respectable unmarried young ladies). A higher education opens the way to the attainment of a respectable occupation such as lawyer, doctor, civil servant, teacher or church official—these being considered exemplary of respectability. Because this is so, and because in many instances education implies wealth, education in metropolitan values, arts and skills is itself a sign of respectability. Thus it may be argued that the two most important institutions which are themselves bastions of respectability, as well as being avenues leading to it, are the church and the school.

Respectability, then, denotes a way of life and a standard of living which, though feasible throughout Caribbean societies, is not authentic to it. Its origin is alien and its values misplaced.

Providencia, though it has never been a colony in the strict sense of the term, does occupy a quasi-colonial status with regard to Colombia. Its people are English-speaking Protestant Negroes living in a basically Spanish-speaking, Catholic, mestizo country. Though not exploited for the benefit of the mainland, Providencia has been virtually ignored and neglected throughout the time of its association with Colombia. Its people have looked to the cultures of the United States, Panama (the Canal Zone) and Jamaica for their own model. Nevertheless, all that we have said about respectability does apply to Providencia.

Respectability, by definition, is exclusive, for the few. Those few consider themselves superior, but their superiority can be measured only against the apparent inferiority of the majority; so it becomes true to say that respectability is seen to have been gained at the expense of that majority. No population can live by negative standards, nor can a majority continue to rest content with an inferior social and moral position. Consequently, throughout the Caribbean, including Providencia, there exists an opposing but politically subordinate value complex through which individuals can achieve a measure of existential fulfillment and recognition. This is reputation.

Reputation is autochthonous, springing from the adaptation of people to local conditions. It is also a counter-culture to respectability and all that respectability stands for. Reputation emphasizes egalitarianism and opposes class hierarchy. It recognizes status differences, but it does not rank one status above another. It regulates social relations by exercising sanctions intrinsic to the relations themselves rather than by invoking external codes of law. A man's reputation is rooted in his fathering of children, which is the most important demonstration of his maturity and manhood. It is the honoring of fatherhood by bearing responsibility for it that is the heart of a man's good name. Arising out of this basic value are numerous other qualities that are prized, and whose attainment contributes to reputation. Among these are a readiness to fight in defense of one's honor and a proficiency in the use of language, notably in sweet talk, word games, riddles, storytelling, punning, boasting, insults, curses—generally being verbally fluent. Closely related to these skills are musical ability and knowledge of local lore such as genealogy, history, local flora and fauna, agricultural and horticultural methods, and particularly fishing and all the lore of the sea, navigation and boats. Carpentry and mechanical skills are also contributory to a man's reputation, while to be able to tell tales of foreign lands or of long voyages enhances the standing of a man among his peers. In reputation it is learning and wisdom that are valued, whereas respectability recognizes education. A man's reputation rests on the extent of his wisdom, but if he wants to become respectable, he needs a certificate.

A man's reputation is relative to that of his peers, there being no absolute standards or abstract criteria of excellence. A man with a reputation for being a good musician is good only with respect to other local musicians—he does not attain to some mysterious absolute standard of supremacy. He can always be bested. Nor is a good musician better than or ranked above a good fisherman. They are equals in all respects but their particular activity.

Like respectability, reputation incorporates a system of moral evaluation and judgment. All men's reputations must be earned and bestowed. They are therefore dependent on recognition. And so we find that of all the moral values upon which social relations depend, that of confidence or trust is perhaps the most important in the Caribbean. One must be able to trust as well as be trusted, and it is this, together with common interest, that structures the peer groups, or crews, that are the sociological basis of male social life in the Caribbean. In turn these peer groups hinge upon the relationship known as "best friend." All men have some measure of reputation, and it is that measure of reputation that gives them a place and a sense of integrity among other men in a community and in a society.

Between reputation and respectability there is a constant struggle in which authority is validated only through reputation, and power granted only through respectability. For example, no official can hope to have his orders or requests properly carried out unless he has some positive reputation among those he is commanding. He does, of course, have the power to enforce his orders, but though respectable, unless he has a reputation, he has no respect.

There are many, and often subtle, ways by which reputation undermines respectability—by noncooperation, by satire, by withholding services, by gossip, by stealing and by deception. In some instances, where political and economic problems have come to a head, reputation and respectability have clashed violently. But the main point to notice here is that reputation and respectability are in a sense dependent on each other: both together make up a single system. The nature of this system is that it is dual and contradictory; every individual must accommodate himself from birth to these contradictions, trying to overcome or to reconcile them. Just as the relationship between these values in the society as a whole is a tense and dialectic one, so their reconciliation by any individual involves tension. And inasmuch as all individuals must cope with this tension, so their lives are touched by contradictory or schizoid circumstances. In living through the situations that give shape to their lives, and through which their lives must be made comprehensible, the people of the Caribbean must become, to varying degrees, schizoid. The reconciliation of this dialectic may take as many forms and be as varied as there are individuals to face it. But there are clearly clusters of solutions, and there is some license to generalize. An outsider, particularly a Euro-American, is bound to see what he can only regard as ambivalence in Caribbean behavior because what he sees is a simultaneous acting out of some of his own mores and habits and their contradictions: for example, an educated, well-dressed man who makes no attempt to hide the fact that he lives with a common-law wife, or a white lady who shuns a black lady that one learns is her first cousin, or perhaps even her sister.

I believe that all colonized peoples have lived to some degree with this burden of ambiguity and that it has greatly contributed to the seemingly schizoid nature of the subordinate and oppressed. As far as individuals are concerned, some manage to reconcile themselves—at least to the extent that simply as persons, not political and economic subjects, they have been able to pass through life on an even keel. But some are overwhelmed. Those who believe in the absolute rightness of respectability, and try to act on that belief, rejecting the realizable goals of reputation in favor of an alien set of values they cannot realistically hope to achieve, are those who, I think, become "schizophrenic."

Oscar is an example of the extreme situation in which the schizoid character of the society in which he lives has become transformed into the schizophrenia of a private individual. Because of this, it is possible to argue that Oscar represents an embodiment of the dilemma of the black man in the white man's world. However, I hesitate to insist on this. I also hesitate to insist that the schizoid nature of the society is the *only* cause of Oscar's behavior. Perhaps it might be better to say that the form which Oscar's behavior took is traceable to the tension between respectability and reputation as I have defined these terms. There are other matters which depend on the particular emotions of those with whom he grew up, as well as on his own predispositions, which must be taken into account if any attempt at a clinically specific diagnosis is to be made.

I have no intention, however, of attempting any such diagnosis. Not only am I not competent to do it, I think that such an approach would destroy what has struck me as so subtle and delicate about the man Oscar. What I do want to do is to try and analyze the salient points of relation between the individual, Oscar, and the society, Providencia.

Oscar was an "outside" child—that is, his father was married to a woman other than his mother, who herself was not married. This is a not-uncommon situation in the Caribbean, and in the system of reputation it carries no stigma. But it is not respectable. Unlike children born in a common-law or regular marriage, however, an outside child tends to be brought up by his mother alone, as Oscar was, or in the presence of a stepfather. Oscar was very close to his mother, and as he grew up, he became the "man about the house." But he also lets it slip that his mother's house became a "cage" for him.

His undeniable intelligence directed his ambitions, which could be realized only in certain culturally directed ways: he could have become a schoolteacher or a church official. The church has long been the only white-originated (hence respectable) institution in the Caribbean through which poor people like Oscar could legitimately fulfill intellectual ambitions engendered by the respectable society—primarily through its schools. Wisdom, especially religious wisdom, is one of the most highly prized achievements of reputation, and through wisdom one theoretically can make the transition from reputation to respectability. Oscar, however, started with three extreme disadvantages—he was black, very poor and an outside child.

The desire to be better than his father—who was a good handyman, but not schooled—provided the immediate impetus for Oscar's ambition. But the man he sought to emulate was his maternal grandfather, Captain John J. Newball, a "genuine" white man who achieved a notably respectable position. Oscar appears to wish to vindicate his mother's degradation—hence his own—at the hands of his father.

But to be literate or even to become a minister of the church is not enough to achieve full respectability. To do this, a man must negate the moral circumstances of his birth and family relationship. This he can do only by marrying legitimately and achieving manhood as a father—which in the Caribbean means not just begetting children, but providing for them. Oscar not only failed in this, he failed miserably. He married out of a misplaced sense of duty to respectability. He got his girl friend pregnant and married her because it was the "right" thing to do. Then she was unfaithful, beginning with when he left the island to begin his training for the ministry. Though she bore him five children, he has lost touch with all of them.

Oscar was brought up a Baptist, but he chose to pursue his ambitions in the Adventist Church. Some of the reasons for this may have to do with his feelings toward his father and mother, who were both Baptists. It is also likely that the more efficient and wealthier educational program of the Adventists, coupled with their greater proselytizing zeal, simply offered him a more real opportunity. The Adventist Church, though, especially on Providencia, includes far more "respectable" upper-class and white members of the society than any other church, and its closed nature—based partially on the unwillingness of its members to go outside the church to solve their difficulties, and their refusal to participate in the ordinary recreational pursuits of the society—makes it appear a somewhat elitist institution. From the outset, then, it was harder for Oscar to move from reputation to respectability through the Adventist Church than it would have been had he sought office in the Baptist or even the Roman Catholic Church.

Oscar was certainly invited to the Adventist Training College in Panama. The question is: In what capacity was he invited? He seems to think he was invited to study for the ministry, but there are also hints in what he says that the officials there employed him as a menial or a gardener.

Just what did happen during his stay in Panama will never be known. But it was there that he broke down, and I suspect it was there that the impossibility of his ever being able to pass from reputation to respectability became apparent to him. And to this failure to be accepted into the ministry was added his failure as a son, as a husband and as a father.

When what are regarded as the superior people of the superior culture endorse a given mode of aspiration and expression and proceed to judge others by it, it is to be expected that those others might measure fulfillment in terms of their success in meeting these expectations. The standards of respectability and its main agent, the church, hold just this place in Caribbean society. But when an individual or a group attempts to meet these standards, he has the right to expect help; and when he achieves the goal, he has the right to recognition. In the Caribbean, however, the Caribbean Englishman never becomes an Englishman, and black is never recognized as white by those who recognize each other as white. Having decided on this course, Oscar may have received help, but he seems to have gained no recognition.

But the extraordinary thing to me is that although bitter about the past, and about himself in the past, Oscar had turned his life into a positive, and one might also say, triumphant campaign. Having been led on by the ambitions engendered by the dominant values of his culture, and then been let down by the keepers of those values, he became a man rejected emotionally, socially and culturally. And yet he managed not only to survive, but came to establish himself in a unique position of dominance, even respect, among the people of Providencia.

Oscar had a reputation that extended beyond the boundaries of Providencia. When I first went to San Andrés, and I told people there I was going to Providencia, they would tell me to look out for Oscar, and then they would laugh. When I pressed them to tell me more, they said he was a madman, but that he was also very intelligent; that he knew all the history of these parts and he knew his people.

When I got to Providencia I was told about Oscar in the same terms, and as I got to know people they would express their opinions in greater detail. I also had the opportunity to see how people's opinions compared with their actions toward Oscar. The initial ambiguity expressed by San Andrésanos and Providencians—that Oscar was both mad and very intelligent—remained unqualified; if anything, the better I got to know people, the greater their ambivalence seemed to be. There was no doubt that even the most highly educated islanders had a considerable respect for him, even if it was a little begrudging. The Baptist minister, for example, while he would laugh at Oscar's excesses and tease him, would in private contemplate deeply on what he thought Oscar was trying to get at with his words. The simpler, less educated people, while they too teased him, remained in some sort of awe of his apparent learning, and not infrequently took to heart some of his condemnation of their behavior. They were also grateful for his gossip. Everyone at some time or other showed him hospitality, and no one really dared to disdain him.

On the other side of their attitude, though, was fear. Oscar was frequently described as being evil, as being the Devil (not a devil). Some thought he knew obeah. Some of the island women seemed genuinely afraid of him and would shut themselves in their houses if they knew he was around. Certainly his ability to appear in a doorway without prior warning could appear uncanny, and his practice of greasing his feet and stealing noiselessly through a house at night, taking some objects and leaving others "in exchange," lent substance to a sort of supernatural quality that people in their fear attributed to him. This sort of fear, however, was more superstition than substance. The real fear—the one which a visitor notices, and which I myself came to experience—goes far deeper and, I think, has far more to do with a condition shared by the entire population, one to which Oscar is related in a rather special way.

I would therefore like to attempt an explanation of

this ambivalent attitude of a population toward one of its members, an individual whom it terms mad, but for whom it has considerable respect; a person it considers intelligent, but whom it fears.

There are two levels at which I wish to offer this discussion: Oscar's use of language, and his behavior with respect to privacy.

> Thus the word is both a sonant object and a vehicle of signification. If you direct your attention to the signification, the world is effaced; you go beyond it and fuse the meaning with the thing signified. If, however, you are exiled from the universe and are attentive only to the verbal body, which is the only reality you can possess and hold between your tongue and lips, then it is the thing signified which disappears and the signification becomes a vanishing of being, a mist which, beyond the word, is in the process of being dissipated.
>
> —Jean-Paul Sartre:
> *Saint Genet, Actor and Martyr*

The Negro people of the Caribbean had the English language forced upon them. But they took it and made it into a language that was not the language of the English people. Each word in Caribbean English carries much more meaning than the same word in American or British English. In early days a white English slaveholder could listen to his slaves speaking English without necessarily understanding what was being said, as slaves frequently meant something other than the obvious signification of the words. The "man of words" became the specialist who fashioned English into a new art form, who made the ambiguities of the language into a language itself. And language itself was fused with other possibilities of communication—with facial expression, with bodily gesture, with tone of voice, with lip and eye movements, and with posture. Under conditions where work was slavery, language became one of the means by which work could be transformed into a modicum of entertainment. For a people deprived of time and access to rest and creative outlets, language was both the tool and the material out of which a variegated store of art and culture could be fashioned. Stories, insults, boasts, toasts, poems, allusions, parables, jokes, irony, satire, mimicry, puns and style evolved to heights and extents unknown to the speakers of English. When these language arts were joined with music, the art of the Caribbean language emerged.

But the English language in the Caribbean has also been a political instrument. White slaveholders forced their slaves to speak English for their own convenience and in support of their own power. For only if there was at least a minimal linguistic basis for understanding could the dominance of the white slaveholder be maintained. To be obeyed, orders must be understood. But the slave took the language and made it his own without the owner realizing it. And he thus succeeded in no small measure in isolating himself from the overbearing white culture. The very language that was forced upon him in order to establish a continuity between the races and cultures became instead a vehicle of discontinuity. The means whereby the white sought to make the Black dependent became the instrument by which the Black came to achieve independence. And because it was still the English language, the English never knew what was going on; the language was the veil of deception. Since it was the Black who initiated this process, he became the deceiver, and it was he who held the initiative. The white man simply took this as further evidence of the black man's inferiority, thereby cutting himself off even more.

Language in the Caribbean is not simply communication; it is also communication about communication, controlled and developed to an art form. And the man of words, the expert, the paragon, the exemplar, is the man who more than any other is the object of his neighbors' esteem.

The strength and wit of Oscar's language earned him respect in the eyes of his fellow-men: as a practitioner of language (as opposed to being a practitioner of politics, medicine, painting, dance or business), he could claim a positive place in the value system of the society, the authentic value system that had evolved in reaction to the dominant but alien system of the whites. Oscar was respected because of his reputation, and his reputation rested on words.

Oscar used words in a way that went beyond the abilities of others on Providencia. He also used them more than others, and though he could not be approached in terms of virtuosity, he could be admired for it at the same time that he was isolated by it. Oscar is a virtuoso, but his virtuosity does not stop at the accepted limits of signification. It goes beyond those limits, and in so doing plays upon language that is already a play.

Oscar's language is not meant to be a simple act of communication; it is a thing in itself. Not just the words have meaning, but the uttering of the words itself has meaning. Yet when someone listens to a person speaking, he naturally expects meaning to come from the speaker's words and the context in which they are used. When Oscar speaks, one looks for meaning in what he is saying. And since Oscar uses a religious idiom, one searches for a message, too. But the meaning and the message are not apparent. They have not been conveyed in the form anticipated by the listener who, knowing he has heard English, cannot believe that what he understands has no meaning. To dismiss what he has heard is to admit his own inadequacy: to accept it is to give it meaning. But one must search constantly for the meaning beyond the actual words. On one level, Oscar is accepted, but much of what he says and stands for is beyond the comprehension of the listener. In this way Oscar isolates himself from the rest, but they remain bound to him by their sense that although the meaning is beyond them, there *is* meaning nevertheless.

Tools have nothing to command or forbid the disintegrated, vagabond element, the wandering individual who is Jean Genet. Of course he is not unaware of them. He has read the notice tacked on the wall, he knows that the mat at the foot of the steps is a request to wipe his feet. In fact he will obey the injunction. But his act is only a feint.

—Jean-Paul Sartre:
Saint Genet, Actor and Martyr

Language is something that Oscar manufactures, or at least something he has taken over and refashioned according to his own design. I am not saying he invents words, but that he takes language as a whole and makes it his tool. Since it is speech rather than the written word that he manipulates, we must bear in mind that it is coterminous with his presence. Oscar and his speech are one and the same; they coexist only as long as he is there. When he has finished talking, his speech evaporates into the memories of his listeners. As soon as he stops talking, Oscar becomes a fantasy, ambiguous and amorphous. He becomes a something that was, and a possibility of something that will be—but no longer a presence. When he is away, one wonders whether he exists. We have him, but we have him not. Upon hearing him, one cannot believe one's ears, and yet one *is* hearing him. When he stops talking, one ceases to have the validation that his words provide.

This elusiveness is illustrated by, indeed embodied in, his wandering behavior. He never stays in one place for any predictable length of time—now one sees him, now he is gone. He can and does move in total silence. He will pass soundlessly through a sleeping house or spend the night underneath a house—your house or mine. One knows that he has been there—therefore, that he is—only by the objects he has left behind.

And what of these objects, the ever-changing contents of his sack or his hat? Sticks, stones, weeds, bottles, fish heads? These are natural objects which have no value aside from their relationship to Oscar; it is he who has invested them with meaning. He steals objects which have value to others: clothes, utensils, books. They have value because they have "paid" their owners by their own utility. In exchange Oscar leaves his objects. They have been collected by Oscar, and his leaving them behind has the value of indicating that he has been there. He makes his presence even more obvious by arranging sticks or pebbles in the form of a cross, an unnatural object.

These objects are like Oscar's language—property so common to all that they are no longer thought of as property. But Oscar's use of them reincorporates them into society; he appropriates them and allows them to stand in his stead. However, since they cannot be used by others, they have no value to them except insofar as they represent Oscar.

The artifacts to which other people attribute value are valueless to Oscar. The artifacts he uses to represent him have *only* this value to others, but they have considerable value to Oscar. Thus what he has done is remove himself from the level at which ordinary people reflect value, even though he has retained the same media (language and artifacts) and the same materials they work with. He is not a foreigner whose language and life products are incomprehensible. He is recognizably one of them, yet at the same time beyond them. His behavior is not an alternative to, but rather a denial of, their own. He establishes his isolation from them at the same time that he forces them to recognize their dependence on him. He steals government documents and then offers to find them (but not the thief). He steals from people objects they want back, but he does not require that they return the objects he leaves in exchange. He delivers a sermon, but does not listen to what other people have to say; in fact, when he is in the position of a listener—as in church—he creates dissonance.

Thus Oscar, unlike Genet, does not obey the injunction and feels no need to feint. He knows that it has meaning for others, but that he has no need of it. Oscar has succeeded in excluding reciprocity, and for Sartre, the exclusion of reciprocity *is* evil, because it is detachment and severance. But Oscar, even though he has succeeded in excluding reciprocity, has only become isolated and neither severed nor detached from the people of Providencia. For in isolation there is still relationship.

Why and how this is so brings us to the discussion of privacy and Oscar's madness.

The two thousand people of Providencia live in fourteen small communities, most of which are no more than fifteen minutes' walk from each other. For nearly two hundred years they have married and mated with each other, so their claim that all the islanders are "one family" is not too far from the truth. The individuals in this population are not only bound together by a dense network of genealogical ties, they have a common life situation and a common historical experience—a single cultural memory. The dualism of the value system has not given rise to a dual society, one which could be said to be split into two population segments which have structural permanence. Everyone faces the strain of reconciling reputation and respectability, rather than opting for one or the other, and the respectable person cannot guarantee the same status to his heirs.

These common bonds and the resultant exclusiveness, which outsiders often see as a stubborn independence and conservatism, make Providencia a closed society. Even though it shares much of its culture with other Caribbean societies, as a living community it is very difficult to break into. Behind the barriers of the closed society, however, is a wide-open way of life. Men conduct their social lives in rum shops or in shady spots on the beach; women work and chat in houses where the doors are always open—if for no other reason than to allow the breezes to circulate—or they gather in a cool corner of the yard. Houses stand close to one another, separated by yards which are often no more than symbolic barriers. Children especially, but also adults, pass freely in and out of yards as well as houses.

The intimacy that is intrinsic to island life makes privacy a delicate and sensitive commodity. Social life is marked by numerous stratagems and tactics whose aim is to secure that privacy which the environment inhibits. Wealthy people, for example, build two-storied houses and live in the upper story. True, this is not just for the sake of privacy, but privacy is a factor. It is hard to come upon a house by surprise because there is always someone—a child, an old man or woman—sitting by the window, on the verandah or in the doorway, partly with the express purpose of keeping an eye out for whoever is coming along the road.

Various devices are used in conversation that allow people, even though they are conversing in the open, to keep what they are saying to themselves. Tones are hushed or a hand is placed in front of the mouth; one puts one's face close to the ear of the listener, or by grasping the elbow one takes someone aside. Even when someone is embarking on the most innocent of journeys, he will very often lay a false trail, or be as noncommittal as possible about his destination. To the inevitable inquiry "Where are you going?" or "What you doing?" one replies, "Taking a walk." And if a boy and girl wish to rendezvous, they set out in opposite directions from each other and from their planned destination.

It is very difficult for anyone to go about his business unobserved, as a hundred pairs of eyes will have watched his progress from one house to another. And the word of his coming may reach his destination before he does, since the island is crisscrossed by narrow overgrown paths along which people (children particularly) run messages. Gossip and warnings get to communities long before officials and other visitors have made their way over the regular paths.

Since the closed society is so open on the inside, it forces a certain degree of secretiveness and stealth upon all its members. But as soon as anyone gives any hint of behaving secretively, curiosity is kindled, and nine times out of ten, people will make an effort to find out what is going on. Gossip and rumor run their inevitable course. Furthermore, everyone at some time or other may be involved in activities which involve these conflicting notions. One may wish at the same time both to do something in private, and to find out what someone else is doing. Much behavior is thus marked by these two inclinations straining against each other.

And yet I do not want to convey that Providencians are people driven to some sort of neurotic frame of mind by an obsession with snooping and hiding. The fact of the matter is that there is a premium on privacy in any small closed community, and this being so, privacy itself stands out as being more important than it

Peter J. Wilson

might ordinarily be in some other, more open community.

Now, if privacy is more important because it is precarious and difficult to achieve, then any factor or person that adds to the basic and inescapable difficulties of maintaining privacy is a nuisance, or even a danger. And like any danger is to be avoided, put off, or if possible, placated.

I think that more than anything else, Oscar's relation to the rest of the society is explicable in these terms: that he is a real and possibly uncalled-for threat to the ordinary everyday privacy of members of the community. At the same time, however, he is a very useful source of news, a revealer of the privacy of others, and in this guise he may be looked upon positively, at least to the extent of being tolerated. In some instances it may even pay to encourage his behavior in order to find out what is going on.

There is, then, at many levels, an ambiguous attitude toward Oscar, stemming from the ambiguity that is inherent in the restrictions on privacy. For example, the crowd's reaction to Oscar's revelation of Joton Campbell's incest was ambivalent. To appear interested and to encourage him would be to condone his behavior. But to ignore what he had to say, or to prevent him from saying it, would be an unnecessary self-denial. When Oscar stole papers from the government offices and hid them in a garbage can, he aroused ambivalence in yet another way. On the one hand, his action served to some extent to express feelings of distrust held by people in general toward the government. On the other, he had committed a burglary. Then there is the problem of Oscar's credibility. If he gossips

134

about someone else, one is more ready to believe him than if the gossip is about one's self—in which case one is anxious to negate him.

How, then, can people "take" Oscar? Especially if they cannot send him off to an asylum? By calling him "mad," while at the same time having reservations about it, the people of Providencia are able to take away from Oscar the power of sanction; they can decide for themselves, as it suits them, whether to believe what he has to say or not. In their eyes, Oscar is not mad all the time; he is sometimes in and sometimes out. Underlying their categorization is the desire to exert some control over his credibility at the same time that they find it useful to accept him and his madness.

There is, I think, more to this relationship of madness, privacy and the daily activity of "normal" people; the fact that Oscar brings out this relationship in an extreme way encourages me to try and expand upon what I have said thus far.

In speaking of privacy I do not mean simply the desire of people to be alone. I understand privacy to mean a situation in which a person may be alone with another person, or alone by himself, but alone in such a way that his relationship with others is not interrupted. Privacy is the condition by which all social relations are fulfilled; it is not so much a psychological need as it is a social need. In order that any given relationship be activated, the participants must suspend or disengage from their other relationships, and the other partners in these other relationships must agree to the disengagement. Privacy, then, is the simultaneous activation of one relationship and disengagement from another. It is, in fact, the basic *relation between relationships;* without it, no individual can function, since it is through relationships that he achieves his sense of identity. Neither can a social system function, since social relations are its elementary components. Understood in this way, privacy is critical to the social life both of individuals and total societies.

The successful activation of any given relationship requires that those concerned disengage themselves, with equal success, from other persons with whom they enjoy relationships, and to whom they are bound. The successful achievement of a relationship and disengagement may be taken as a measure of the *authority* a person has over himself, but with respect to others. Some relationships, notably those we regard as intimate, require a greater degree of disengagement from other relationships, and any inability of those intimately related to keep others out easily indicates their loss of authority. Conversely, it is the measure of *power* of persons that in some way or other they can prevent those to whom they are related from acting with others. Thus in privacy lies the roots of social power and authority.

I think it can be appreciated that Oscar's ability to invade and intrude upon the privacy of others, to intercede in the relationships they seek to pursue, is an indication of the power he exerts over them. In this sense there is something of the tyrant about Oscar. I know from my own experience the extent to which this power can be quite overwhelming. My wife and I were at times driven to furtiveness in even the most innocent aspects of our relationship, even when we were within the privacy of our island home. The people of Providencia have to live with this day in and day out, year in and year out, while I always knew I would be leaving. A tremendous power lies in the potential to invade privacy; in this case, that power was wielded by Oscar. Like all exercises of power it generates fear in those who are its objects.

Normally the threat of this power is kept in bounds by the reciprocity of trust, discretion, respect and honor. But Oscar excludes reciprocity. He does not observe the conventions of trust and honor. One can never know that what Oscar has learned he will not pass on—he might, or he might not. Such then is the basis of the power he is able to exercise over people, a power which at the same time threatened to undermine their authority over themselves.

Oscar himself never engaged in any sustained relationship with others. It was he who initiated and terminated all contacts. He excluded reciprocity. He came to me when he wanted to, and not if I asked him (though he *might* come if I asked). He told me what he wanted me to hear. He left when he felt like it. He worked for others as a sugar boiler when he wanted to, but he worked for whoever he wanted to, not for whoever wanted him. He divulged secrets when he saw fit, but not when others asked him. He begged or borrowed when he needed, but if no one would give him what he wanted, he would steal it—even though he called it exchange. In other words, he more or less effectively prevented anyone else from exercising any power over him. And he maintained a more or less absolute authority over himself. Oscar's life was so wholly public that he had no domain of privacy through which other people could strike a balance of power with him. Or to put it another way, his privacy was so complete that no one could gain access to it in order to erode his authority. And yet he remained a social being: he entered into relations with others, but withdrew at will; he could still communicate with others, when he chose. And possibly, at least to the barest minimum, he was still beholden to them.

I should perhaps make it clear that I am trying to describe the present situation, the situation in which Oscar exists for others as a madman. In his earlier life, before he broke down, it is clear he recognized privacy; in fact, it was the erosion of his privacy, the determination by others of his relationships, which led to his collapse. The present situation, however, seems to be one by which he has climbed out of his earlier defeat and has transcended the very framework of social behavior to achieve a unique position among his fellows.

But why madness? For that matter, what is madness? In part I would say that it comprises the abrogation of relations with other people which gives rise to such complete authority that they are rendered powerless. The only recourse available to those who are so overwhelmed is to banish such tyranny from their lives—to a hospital, an asylum, any ship of fools. Such banishment is accomplished emotionally and rationally by conferring the label "madness," for in one word the individual is deprived of responsibility; hence, there is no need to recognize him. Madness, then, is tyranny, and it seems to be in the nature of tyranny that it comes to be madness: Nero, fiddling while Rome burns? Mad! Hitler flying into rages, not listening to his generals? Mad! Senator McCarthy finding communists in every nook and cranny? Mad! The more absolute we see the exercise of power to be, the more our only recourse for regaining authority is to push that power outside the normal frame of reference.

But privacy as I am talking about it here is part of everyman's life and day-to-day behavior. In this nonpolitical sense Oscar seems to represent in his person, and in his relations with the people of the island, the development to an extreme degree of this tension of privacy. Normally this tension is well accommodated, but the moment it teeters off course it can begin to pose enormous threats to social life.

The gravity of this threat rests not only in its disruption of social life itself, but in the distortion of an individual's sense of himself. Contemporary psychologies, and certain philosophies too, are agreed that for each and every human being a sense of identity is a *sine qua non* of existence. In modern life the achievement of this identity, of the being-for-oneself and the being-for-others, has become increasingly difficult because of the proliferation of alienating and fragmenting institutions and patterns of living. And this difficulty has converted *identity* into a *problem* of identity. However, it is surely true to say that the search for identity has always been a task for all individuals in every culture. Now the task has been made more difficult than at any other time.

The search for identity rests squarely on the freedom of choice we can exercise in entering into and conducting relationships with others. By seeking total divorce from others we can achieve nothing except complete alienation and total negation; in fact, as Oscar's story illustrates, the achievement of pure self-autonomy is sheer madness, the denial that one is recognizable by others. Thus I would argue that the idea of self-control is to be understood as control of oneself in respect of others. Its exercise and achievement must be contingent on the submission and assent of others, as their self-control is dependent on our submission. Let us take this general argument as it applies to privacy.

If I achieve a state of privacy—that is, if I choose the time, place and person of my relationship—then I am dependent on the willingness of those others to whom I am bound in some way to leave me alone, to respect my privacy. But suppose they do not respect me, and do not leave me alone? Suppose they interfere, intrude, interrupt or even prevent by force my preferred and chosen association? In doing this they prevent me from satisfying myself in respect of the other I have chosen, and have been chosen by. My integrity has been shattered and my freedom usurped. My authority not only with respect to others, but over myself, has been undermined.

Why should others not let me alone? One reason is that they do not trust me. They do not believe that in my chosen relationship I will not in some way or other pose a threat to their own relations to me and thence erode their own authority. But in what sense can this be?

Well, if others are as dependent on me for recognition as I am on them, then is not my separation from them in some measure a withdrawal of my recognition, potentially if not actually? To take an extreme example: Why cannot the lover bear to be parted from the beloved, especially if the beloved is with someone else? If separation requires trust, then in separation there must be grounds for mistrust, for every relationship that a partner undertakes may modify every other relationship in which he is involved. And the more I succeed in keeping others out, the more I enhance my authority while challenging their power by withholding my recognition. Equally, the more susceptible my own relationships are to the interference of others, the greater their measure of power over me, and the less my authority.

One can't help suggesting that what we do in the ordinary course of everyday life is accommodate to each other by striking some sort of balance. But at the same time, thinking of it this way suggests that there must be some limits beyond which trespass can only have the direst consequences. If an individual or a group erects more and more impenetrable barriers to surveillance by others, then the threat to others' power becomes intolerable, and in the extreme situation, these others may be driven to irrational and violent reaction —to witch hunts, inquisitions and other forms of blind violence. Historically, this has resulted in the darker times that, when we look back, we call "mad." Or when the power of those to whom we are bound becomes so irresistible that our privacy shatters about us, then we are driven to conspiracy, secrecy, plotting, anarchy. And "madness."

Privacy and surveillance, as many have pointed out, are two sides of the same coin, and each contributes to the existence of the other. There is no need here to enter further into the sociological and political implications of the argument. I am concerned to point out that when we call a man "mad," we acknowledge that by the evidence of his behavior he has reached a point at which he is beyond our power to control. We submit to him, for he achieves a complete authority over us while we are unable to make even a dent in his self-control. Since we are not willing either to admit to impotence or submit to slavery, the only way out for us—apart from complete annihilation—is to disqualify the threat by calling it "madness." It seems to be this situation that the relationship between Oscar and the people of Providencia throws into relief, although I am not saying that they have reached this point of no return.

Oscar and the people of Providencia appear to have worked out a compromise to overcome the threat that was posed. By recognizing that they have a relationship with each other, both Oscar and the people of the island guard and grant each other their freedom through their privacy, even while they have agreed to give up some of what "normal" people may reasonably expect of each other.

About the Author

PETER J. WILSON is a British anthropologist who has taught in the United States at Bennington College and at Yale. He is currently associate professor of anthropology at the University of Otago, Dunedin, New Zealand. He is author of *Crab Antics: The Social Anthropology of English-Speaking Negro Societies of the Caribbean* (Yale, 1973).